# Conclave

# Spring 2016

# Conclave

Spring Issue
First Edition
Copyright © 2016
Published by The Balkan Press
All rights reserved

**Editor-in-Chief**: Lara Bernhardt
**Associate Editors**: Kadey Bernhardt, Alice Bernhardt
**Publisher**: William Bernhardt
**Editors Emeritus**: Savannah Thorne, Valya Dudycz Lupescu
**Cover Art & Design**: Hien Chau, Brian Roe
**Advisory Council:**

| | | |
|---|---|---|
| Tracey Thompson | Ken Somerset | Tom Stoerzbach |
| Brenda G Thomas | Bill Wetterman | Jaz Primo |
| RJ Johnson | Amanda Sullivan | Sue McMurphy |
| Nikki Hanna | Michael Blaschke | Cheri White |
| Deborah Harris | Deborah D. Wilson | Robert Silberstein |
| Dorraine Darden | Betty L. Perkins | William Bonney |
| Deborah Bouziden | Elaine Gallant | John Wooley |
| Gregory Field | Renee Roberts | Tim Foley |
| Selma Mann | Rick Ludwig | William Fernandez |
| Anthony L. DeWitt | Lori Bogedin | Yvonne S. Kaiser |
| Randy Goodman | Al Mertens | Kenneth Andru |
| Connie Suttle | Nicholas Soleyn | |

# Conclave

Writing for Change
Spring 2016

# BALKAN PRESS

## A Note From the Editor

"Nothing in life is certain but death and taxes."

No one argues with Dr. Franklin's famous adage. But I'd add another certainty: change. The very nature of our world results in continual change. Day to night, month to month, season to season, year to year. Nothing stays the same. We age, we adapt, we cope. And just when we think we have everything under control, some new change yanks the rug out from under us.

In this world of uncertainty, writers share their experiences, share how they cope with difficulties, with change. They let others know they are not alone in their struggles. Writers shine a beacon to light the path. Writers can also bring about change by sharing their outrage. History provides countless examples of positive change brought about by excellent writing. Charles Dickens' stories of crushing poverty. Upton Sinclair's indignation over meat-packing conditions. Thoreau's game-changing concept of civil disobedience. Positive change brought about by excellent writing.

For our first issue of *Conclave*, we wanted to focus on change— change of mind, change of heart, change of guard, change of spirit, change for the betterment of every precious soul on earth. So we invited writers everywhere to send us passionate writing about change. I hope you will be as pleased with and as excited by the results as I am.

Change can be scary. But change also can be exciting and necessary and good. And change is certain. Working together, we can do our best to shepherd and safeguard the future. And then we will welcome those changes with open arms.

Lara Bernhardt, Editor-in-Chief

# Contents

# Waves

Toti O'Brien

I have tried for years not to fall into what seemed a kind of childish trap: being more struck by close tragedies than by distant ones. Logic and experience have shown me tragedies are of two kinds: those occurring to me and those not. Between such non-communicating zones there is discontinuity: we can't go from one to the other a step at a time. There's no ladder. They are entities of different nature: they cannot be added, subtracted, multiplied.

When a catastrophe strikes you directly, you have to cope with all manner of unwanted change, with substantial revising of your existence—or the loss of it. Consequently you are transported into a separate sphere where—though others can be of help or comfort—you are all by yourself.

When a tragedy occurs to others, they are propelled into the abovementioned bubble where—though exceptionally you could be of help or comfort—you will not have access. Those two areas of loneliness, as I said, do not touch.

I am irked by my tendency of being more struck by some disasters than others: such an attitude seems unjustified.

I lack impartiality. Some events move me in a deeper way: clearly, conscious or unconscious identification is a stake. Circumstances either cause me to identify with those directly concerned (with the effect of mirroring, at various degrees of intensity, their conditions, their feelings) or they make me re-live traumas that—in the past—have affected my intimate sphere (me, my son, my dog, my parrot, my car, my kite or my doll). Reasoning along such lines seems correct. By which I mean it correctly diagnoses my improper response.

Sometimes, geographically or chronologically remote circumstances have a mighty resonance. More commonly, closer ones do. Not too long ago, a plane crushed by the Indonesian coast around Christmas obsessed me with grief. Why so powerfully, while equally horrifying things filled the news?

Equally: here's the point. Circumstances involving the damaging of massive quantities of humans—or a few, even one individual, massively damaged—should provoke a same response at the emotional and the intellectual level. Unless, obviously, we break into the other category: when things happen to you - your son, your parrot, your car, your house or your dog.

Recently the Paris shooting of November, 2015, then the killing in San Bernardino, California, in December, caused me to reflect.

I lived in Paris a large part of my life. I still have strong ties to the city. After the news broke, I spent anguished hours attempting to reach friends and family, until everyone's safety was ascertained. At that point my body and my brain pleaded: "Could we sigh and relax?" I was struck by my own incongruity. Yes: my fistful of loved ones was unscathed, then what? Should I celebrate? Was there anything, truly, to be happy about? Is happiness allowed, with grief bursting next door? I was stuck in a state of suspension—incapable of savoring relief.

Then, in front of the mediated reactions to the event, I could not help a wave of resentment–kind of a counter-feeling to my initial worry and pain. Too wide a majority was draping itself with the French flag. Too many metaphorically attended the funerals, bluntly ignoring other tragedies going on elsewhere.

Why such a disproportion in the way a western, educated, informed audience reacted to the massacres (aka, killing of civilians) simultaneously happening in different parts of the world? Why did the majority cry solidarity with the Paris' victims, seldom mentioning those who—at the same time—died in Beirut, Kenya,

Nigeria? Was it because these people (Western, mediatized, etc.) more easily identified with a Parisian crowd than with a Lebanese or African one? Of course. Back to square one: closer tragedies also seem graver.

But they aren't. Tragedies are of two kinds only. Ours: and we have to cope. Others': and we'd better not cause them. We might help, sometimes. But we are not supposed to rate them, pick our favorite.

Whoever took the time to look at the pictures, in those November days, must have seen how similar France, Nigeria, Lebanon, Kenya appeared in the light of disaster. Let's say few took the time: the amount of information we can absorb has its limits. Let's say we reacted superficially and Paris resonated, for most Westerners, as a more familiar reality. We, of course, grieved emphatically the familiar, not—or less—the unfamiliar. We reacted on a register of identity, not of humanity.

Are those concepts separate? It depends on how you form the first one. What you identify with, and in which occasions.

Life, death, suffering, justice, should belong in the "humanity" field. They are shared among all, while language, habits, fashion, eating, rules of conduct, and credos are shared within defined communities. Life, death, illness, captivity, violence are issues crossing all borders. But we are prone to consider them only when they are suffered by our kin, so defined on the basis of less universal features. We ignore the predicament of the others. That equates to dividing humanity into those whose suffering matters, those whose doesn't.

Obviously, the reverse applies. Why should those whose suffering doesn't matter to us care about our pain? Should they owe us a respect we do not think they deserve? How could we expect not to be targeted by people whose killing we so scarcely mind, we don't even mention it? While, of course, we cry out loud for our victims.

"Our," in the case of Paris, means more recognizable. It doesn't yet mean "on our side," that would be another scenario.

After the Paris shooting, Pope Francis defined our present state as a "piece meal World War III." Wars have casualties on both sides, and each side counts its own. Enemies do not grieve dead enemies: they keep score and they celebrate. Should enemies start to grieve enemies, the war logic would crack in a blink. Enemies grieving enemies would be called deserters or traitors.

Not to grieve—not to mention—massacred Lebanese, Kenyans, Iraqi civilians, or refugees, equates ranging those victims into enemy territory. It means tracing a line that is, obviously, reversible. The reciprocal becomes true.

The overblown reaction to the Paris shooting, paired by a kind of hysterical blindness in front of equal tragedies, simultaneously happening elsewhere, slapped me in the face, hurting me just as needed. Waking me up.

I was then surprised by the San Bernardino killing: the way it shook me at the core. Was it because it happened next door? My son (dog, car, parrot)... My son gave the news while he drove back from the area. I had been to the exact location, for work, not too long before.

Proximity. I could have been a victim. My son could have been one. The dead might be someone I've seen, met, known. Does it make horror greater? More significant?

Does a close-by tragedy (or a distant one that—whatever the cause—prompts identification) raise our consciousness of tragedy at large, so that when people in the other (physical or mental) hemisphere are struck, we'll be more apt to understand? If we see something break under our eyes, do all events of the same kind become more vivid, more readable? I'm afraid things don't work that way. On the contrary, I fear we tend to circumscribe, reduce, wrap our feelings around what we can touch, erasing the rest: after all there's so much information we can absorb. We are human.

I've tried to treat the San Bernardino shooting with the same distress I'd reserve to any shooting, anywhere, without giving it privileged status. I know there could be objections to my point. It could be argued that each sad affair should be grieved by the closest witnesses (how close? spatially? would a passer-by count?), then all would be, and grief would even itself on the planet. The proximity-logic has risks. Those who destroyed lives in San Bernardino came from afar, and that eased their task.

I've tried to even myself in regard of this next-door shooting. I let its vibration shake, shake still, then slowly wind down. It took time. So I thought of waves.

Just think of the particles tossed around by the explosions. The vibrations caused by the screams of victims and witnesses, by the cries of the bereaved. The olfactory waves: molecules impacted by the smell of powder, of blood, by the sweat of fear and pain. I am not stepping into the metaphorical realm: I am talking reality. Horror can't just erupt then remain, without traveling. There's an epicenter—there must be concentric circles. The commotion bursts then it expands. It cannot be stopped: we are invested, the closest the strongest.

Then the waves, obviously, weaken: the farthest away are the lightest. Are we, thus, *materially* impacted by what happens in our vicinity? Is our body concerned and modified? If such is true, there are degrees of tragedy. If the pain of others tangibly scratches our skin (reaches—even so slightly—our receptors, changes our hormonal balance, alters our magnetic field) before it dissolves, we are more touched when we are more reachable, and that can't be avoided.

## CONCLAVE

Perhaps.

Still, there's that thing we call imagination. We have such power... We can figure what happens far away among those who apparently don't resemble us, aren't like us. We can figure out a link, find a spark of experience we can relate to. We can travel the waves, expand them, ride them. We can reflect—not only on what fits our pocket mirrors, our small reading glasses. We are human.

## Confrontation
Robert Fillman

He had slapped her before.
She spoke from the top
of the stairs, anyway,
while he was still in earshot—
his thin, muscular body
leaning a little to one side,
his good ear toward her,
a strong, square hand stiff
on the rail of the landing,
she, staring down at him for once,
her knotted scarf a burst of red
puffing around her throat,
arms folded tight
like a great spider waiting
for the faintest tremor of her web.
Compared to him
she was still young:
an elastic hourglass
in a black dress,
curves that flirted
without her knowledge.
He could smell the honey of her
blooming in the air
between them, wanted
to launch himself toward her,
instead he contracted.
I will not come down to you,
she promised, as her eyes
narrowed and lips thinned.
Stunned, and with a light

## CONCLAVE

touch of courtesy, he smiled
at his adversary. Bested,
he swallowed the few words
he had been storing in his throat
and slipped out the door
to get wood for the stove.

## All You Need Is Hate
Kenneth Pobo

I'm sure that I hate you
and I carry a gun.
Your religion stinks too.

I know what I should do,
shoot to kill, just for fun.
I'm sure that I hate you—

are you scared? Hope so. Boo!
I panic everyone.
Your religion stinks too,

whatever it is. Screw
your whole group. Better run!
I'm sure that I hate you,

maybe you always knew
you lost big and I won.
Your religion stinks too—

it's all gobbledygoo.
I've got it cocked. You're done.
I'm sure that I hate you.
Your religion stinks too.

## Afghan Women Poets
Jim Bohen

The radio report said that Afghan women poets who aren't
allowed to appear in public by their male relatives, must phone
in their poems in to a meeting of their fellow female poets.
Most Afghan women poets must use pen names to try
to avoid the stones and shards of a morality that's good
at flinging screaming death, indiscriminate pain.

American poets take their kids to soccer games, birthday
parties and the ice cream store. We shop and socialize,
write what we want, wear something provocative,
complain loudly that life isn't fair.
Afghan women poets must decide whether
to leave their homes forever when male elders
threaten death for what they consider immoral poems.
Here, what those Afghan women poets write is
free to be ignored, as most poetry is.
There, the same words can mean death.

One Afghan poet left her rural town because
she wants a life where she can express herself.
She says she's willing to die a dignified death
(which could be anything but)
rather than thumb herself under,
a voice denied, a life suppressed, a spirit caged.

Her courage makes me feel small, makes me ask questions.
Why do we let things like this happen?
Short of guns and bombs and boots on the ground,
can anything be done to end this?

12

How can people live this way, denied what we
consider a given, a birthright almost as basic as breathing?

How can they live with death as a next-door
neighbor who can drop in for tea at any time,
and  splatter the walls with guts and brains?
Because that's how it's always been?
Because there is no choice?

As inertia starts to regain control of my brain,
the translation of a phrase by one Afghan woman poet
rattles my detachment and reverberates inside my skull:

*My country is burning; my heart is on fire.*

**Forensic Foraging I**
William Crawford

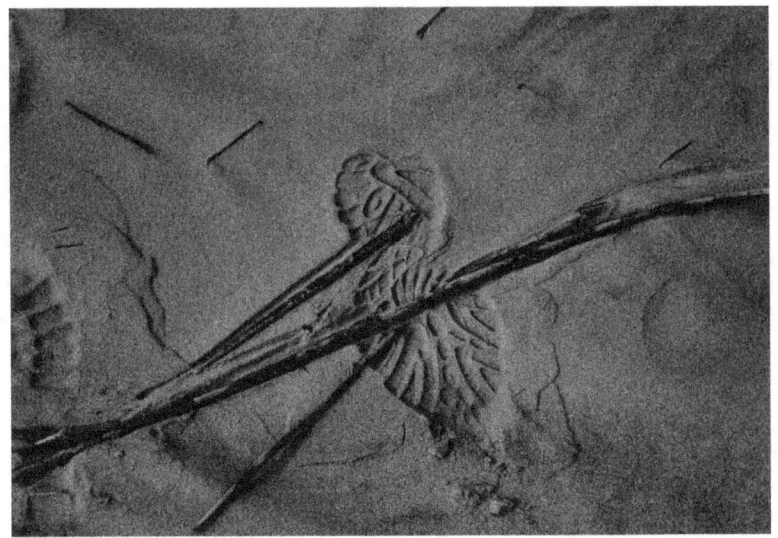

**Forensic Foraging II**
William Crawford

**Forensic Foraging III**
William Crawford

**Forensic Foraging IV**
William Crawford

## The Key
Marjorie Stelmach

You can cobble together
a metaphor
from the most unpromising
scatter. Take, for example,
this maple key.
Its myriad cousins
clog my gutter, clutter
the cracks
of my sidewalk, litter
the birdbath and feeder, cling
to the cat.
They say it takes
ten thousand seeds to make
one tree.
Discouraging odds.
But today, all it takes
is this: pick a key,
any key,
and imagine a craft
whose hold is a cup
of sustenance squirrelled
for the journey:
nourishment, ballast,
moisture enough
to quench a thirst
on your eventual
desert island,
and a lacework sail
to catch
the gale-force winds

that will cast you ashore,
where, like Crusoe,
you'll, little by little, drain
your hold
of its holdings, until
all stores spent
and home a vision
too vague to sustain you,
you come to see
you must give up.

But it's only now
you see the lengths
you'd go to keep
your grip on even
so meager a plot
as this: barely
enough for a grave.
But what a grave!
Envision it: a leafy shade
where a friend might come
to recall your valor,
your pluck,
find solace in the thought
of the nearly
ten-thousand futures
waiting
in the wings,
each one
an adventure worth
the singing. Yes,
a person can cobble a myth
out of almost nothing.

## CONCLAVE

The key
is the dying.

# The Woman Taken in Adultery
Marjorie Stelmach

Years of men's voices speaking of need, speaking
of cost. Or not speaking at all, but reaching, taking.

Brief meetings, crossings where coins change hands—
and nothing else changes.

Decades of this before the stones drop in the dust
from those fists, and a voice says Woman—, says Go—

After which, silence falls.


The parable ends the same way for us, no matter
what words were written in that dust already dispersing,

or written in her heart, or later on her grave,
or written, mis-written, on his cross.

And we, too, must go—
But where? And what will become of us now?

To be fair, he is not told, either.


Nothing shifts in this world. We are sent on our way
into dust, from which, if meaning lifts,

it dissolves, undelivered.
It's all illegible anyway, every transaction.

## CONCLAVE

Needs still unmet.
Costs still uncounted.

Nothing can shift the stone from this story's ellipsis.

## The Seamstress
*after Edward Hopper*
Robert Fillman

In a straight, unforgiving chair
facing a second-floor window
she works upright at her machine.

The sharp slant of the morning sun
beats against skin, white washes arms,
threatens to stitch her eyes shut.

The entire bedroom is aflame
with color lusting from flesh-velvet
wallpaper, the rays of the sun

casting a diagonal cross
on the northern wall behind her.
She wants to let her hair unspool

past her shoulders as she watches
the up and down of the needle.
In white linen, her hands folded

on the desk as if in prayer,
she guides fabric slowly without
a pattern, never losing faith,

her left foot pumping the treadle,
almost expecting organ pipes
to tremble as she threads the seam.

# The Price of Fruit
Maria Elena B. Mahler

It's cold in here. Where am I? The old man. I was thirsty. I couldn't catch my breath. *Diablos. La Migra.* They will want to interrogate me. There are no windows around. Maybe, I'm in some kind of isolation room. Why is it so cold in here? *Ay, Dios mio!* If deported, I'll have to do this all over again . . . I hope not. I cannot do this again.

My body doesn't feel the same. I must be getting old.

Ernestina is waiting for me. I promised her I'd be back in Yuma. Three weeks. But, *ay Dios*, what a time I had with my family. I miss them already. My country is so beautiful. *Viva Mexico! Viva Nayarit!* I can't believe I let twelve years go by without seeing everyone. Ernestina warned me. She didn't want me to leave. "I'll be back before you have time to sigh again," I told her. Her knowing, black eyes were full. She knows my family, my brothers, how we love to eat and drink. *Viva el pulque!*—that heavenly fermented agave sent by the Aztec gods. Thank you God. *Y la Virgencita de Guadalupe también!* I wish they had the good stuff here. I'd never get any work done. I'd be under the shade of a sage bush laughing and caressing my Ernestina all day long. *Mi mujer.* I miss her. Too much *pulque* and partying every day. I haven't had time to think about my woman. I know she wanted children. My sister-in-law ate the lucky carrots. Popped out a dozen wild-running *chiquillos* like a rabbit. My Ernestina, heart of a mother for everyone. Our small house is filled with little ones from our neighbors. Ernestina takes good care of their children after school. *Los papitos* are happy. More work at the end of the day. Extra money for *la familia en México. Ay, Dios!* My Ernestina. Her bony hips. So shy about her body.

"I look like a raisin," she said when I stared, when I passed my hand over her. Over my queen, my beautiful queen of Nayarit. That night I won't forget. Never. Independence Day. A feast of drinking and eating to the rhythm of mariachis and *rancheritas*. We were all so young. Our skin glowed sitting around the fire under the stars. A couple brave friends played love songs and made us cry. I wanted to love. I wanted to feel being loved. Touched by *a girrrrrrrl*. I, the only *burro romanticón*, sitting alone, staring with wet eyes, sparks from the fire disappearing into the night sky—*sólo* with my heart wanting. My brothers with their girlfriends. Ahhhhh, the entanglement of flesh and kisses. One after another rolled slowly, discreetly over the dry grass away from the fire. Through the flames I saw her silhouette approaching. So graceful. She smiled as she passed by my side. The soft red glow behind her revealed her figure through her white skirt and embroidered blouse. I knew in that very instant she was the angel I met so often swimming in the warm lake of my dreams. Bewitched by her soul, my eyes danced to her tune as her skirt danced side to side. My hat lifted from my head, and like a feather, her warm fingers gently stroked my hair. Then she ran laughing and disappeared into the dark. Stupefied by her long black hair flowing in rhythm with her hips, I stared into the darkness with my jaw hanging and my mind wanting to smack myself for not running fast enough behind her. *Idiota. Qué pendejo!* I couldn't rid myself of her enchantment. I never did. She'd been crowned Queen of Nayarit that night—she was merely seventeen. Thank God, days later by the lake, we ran into each other again. She was wearing my hat and told me she was going to return it to me one of these days. I think she was actually following me. At least I hoped she was. I was hers, then and forever. Oh, those sweet days! Endless summer nights filled with music and stars, lost in the forest of citrus blooms. How could I have resisted her olive skin, soft and sweet as mango.

She's still my beautiful queen and love. She thinks she's shrinking into an old dry woman. I never saw the raisin face she talks about when she stands in front of the mirror and pulls her cheeks towards her ears. My love for her is beyond age. Besides, she's not old at all. My mother is old. And my father is older, close to one hundred! Who knows if God will let me see them alive again. *Quién sabe?*

Eva Cruz wakes in the middle of the night coated with sweat—nothing unusual for a summer night on the outskirts of Yuma in a trailer-house without air-conditioning. She quietly sits up against the headboard not wanting to disturb her husband. She runs her hands through her moist black hair. She lets out a breath as she reaches for the night clock turned away towards the wall. Its green numbers are the only light in her pitch-black room. The phone keeps ringing in the distance. *Ay, Dios! I wasn't dreaming.* The cold tile-floor against the bottom of her feet wakes Eva up as she softly rushes to the phone.

"Hello?"

"Hello ma'm," a dry male voice greets back. "Sorry to disturb you. I need to speak with José Cruz."

"Who's this?"

"I just need to speak with José Cruz. I know it's late, but is he there?"

"Look mister! I will not wake up José unless you tell me your name and what you want'm for. It's more than late; it's after three in the morning!" Her voice is firm but she manages to keep her tone low.

"Ma'm, I'm calling from the general hospital in El Centro. My name is Felipe Santos. I'm a nurse looking after a patient here. We need Mr. Cruz to identify him. The patient has no form of identification, except this phone number."

"*Ah, ya entiendo.* Ok. One minute, please. I'll wake my husband."

At dawn, Eva and José Cruz drive their old Pontiac west along the straight and flat highway to El Centro. On any other day, José would be driving east over the Fortuna Mountains and towards Maricopa, where he has worked in the fields for the past eight years.

Eva sits quietly next to her husband, but her mind, like a slot machine spinning for cherries to line up, spits out names of friends and people who could have carried their phone number. Looking through the window, her eyes become lost in the strange forms of human-looking cactus that pass by. *Who is it?* One name after another pops up over the candidates standing in the dry sea.

During the one-hour trip, Eva and José continue without exchanging a word or a look between them. Both are lost in a game of dodging names like landmines.

"I hope it's nothing too serious." Eva breaks the tedious silence as they arrive. "Did the man give you any details of the person's condition?"

"Eva, I already told you all he said. Why don't we go inside and find out." José doesn't look at his wife as he struggles to conceal the uneasiness gurgling in his bowels.

The hospital visitor's parking lot is almost empty. The sun's heat, trapped for months inside the asphalt, makes Eva's heels sink. The heaviness in her feet causes her to lag behind her husband. José waits for her under the porch at the main entrance protecting his head from the glaring desert sun—upset that in their early morning rush he left his straw cowboy hat sitting next to his lunch-box.

Side-by-side, they walk through the corridor to the patient wing with steps echoing against bone walls. Eva's heels stick to the immaculate tiles, leaving behind a serpent of black dots all the way to the reception area. The chubby nurse at the front desk greets them with a smile.

# CONCLAVE

"Good morning. Can I help you?"

The steam from her coffee cup rises like a ghost between her and the newly arrived visitors. Eva and José look at each other wondering who is going to speak first.

"Early this morning I received a call from a nurse. He asked me to come here to identify a patient. Let me see . . . I wrote the nurse's name on a piece of paper." José struggles to find the wrinkled name inside his jeans' pocket. "Felipe Santos?"


Why are they keeping me here so long? They should have thrown me back already. I've lost all sense of time. I don't remember much of what happened. What's today? Let me see. Saturday. I arrived in Los Algodones. The bus ride from Nayarit to the border took over eighteen hours. I slept some. Drank my beer. Ate the tacos my sister made for my ride. They were delicious and juicy from the leftover *chivo asado* from my farewell party. In Los Algodones I waited for the night. Saturday or Sunday are the best nights to cross. At least I have been told so. Twelve years since the first time I crossed. Time can pass quickly, more than we realize. I was much younger. My belly didn't stick out like a big watermelon. That first time, I prepared myself pretty good. I followed the instructions of my cousin Juan. He crossed over a few months earlier without trouble. The desert dunes in mid-March were beginning to warm. The gentle night breeze felt as soft as Ernestina's nightgown against my face. I remember. I just followed the stars. I was crossing into the Promised Land, the land of opportunities! I had bottles of water in every pocket. Carried a small *morral* with more water and a sandwich—it was exhilarating. Ernestina followed months later. She couldn't stand waiting in Nayarit for me to send money. "We'll always be together, in hell or in paradise," she said when we next reunited and hugged for hours. The only thing that mattered was that we were together, standing

28

on American soil. Years have gone by so fast since that sweet moment. Time is strange. Here I am again at the border. While sitting on a bench in the small plaza in Los Algodones, I heard rumors about some women and small children caught the night before. I put out my antennas, went to the corner bar to hear more news. I drank more beer, found out from the bartender that the border was infested with immigration patrols. *Perros. Muchos perros.* He told me these past months *La Migra* has been horrible. I believed him. The cold Tecate didn't quench my thirst.

"Every day people are caught." He continued after pouring himself a shot of Cuervo tequila. "Last month a couple was shot." He didn't know if they made it alive or not. He warned me not to cross on Saturday because of *La Migra*. It becomes evil. Most deaths happen on Saturday nights. More than any other day. *Chupacabras.* I kept drinking. We talked a lot for the rest of the day and I stayed until the bartender closed the bar late after midnight. Since I had no bags, not even a toothbrush, I went back to my bench in the plaza and passed out until the birds in the early morning sang loud above my head. It was impossible even to pretend to be asleep. The hours that Sunday were longer than any other Sunday I can remember. With nothing to do but wait, I read the paper. My throat was dry. It dried even more when I read about two young children captured the night before—mad Saturday. Two girls from Guatemala aimlessly walking in the sand, lost for more than four days. In the black and white pictures they looked ill and starved and only an arm's reach from the dark angels. *Pobrecitas muchachas.* Sunday was the night! I ate the whole day to fill my reserves. I didn't know when I would eat again. I drank a dozen or more beers. *Ay, Dios!* What a heat and no breeze! I was glad I didn't cross the night before. I kept wondering what on earth made *La Migra* patrol so mad on those nights. If I were them I probably would be mad too. On Saturday night, I'd rather be with my wife or at the bar drinking. I'm sure they're pissed off to have to drive through the desert to hunt down a handful of stubborn, hard-skinned *cholos* trying to reach *La Tierra Prometida*.

They take it out on us. We're responsible for their late night work. We ruin their weekends. Truth is, they shouldn't complain and make us pay. Really! They get paid *pretty good*. I'm sure weekend pay is double. *Bastardos! Hijos de la ching . . .* Without us, 'Gringos' would never eat any strawberries. Who would break their backs from sun up to sun down, on four legs, digging out roots and carrots from the dirt? Ahhhh, what's the point of getting mad. It only increases my blood pressure. We just have to play the game. We need them and they need us.

What was I thinking about? *Ay, Dios*, my memory is foggy. I feel this huge dark cloud floating in front of my brain . . . Oh, I said good-bye to my new friend at the bar. *Adiós, compadre. Buen viaje.* He told me. We didn't exchange names. He probably doesn't want to read in the paper the next day that the illegal he just made friends with was hunted down or killed. He gave me a strong two-handed shake. Our eyes sealed the stamp of brotherhood. I remember that! He locked the bar and walked away in the opposite direction of the border. I stood for a while in front of the metal curtain to his bar. I watched him leave under the dim light of the street. I left in the direction towards *la linea*. The night felt calm, quiet, except for a bunch of dogs fighting over a piece of garbage. I had nothing to throw to scatter them. I picked up a small stone instead and threw it. *Pinches perros!* They all ran away. I was alone. The streets were empty. I followed a small street east to the edge of town. From there I followed the border fence into the dark. I crawled from bush to bush along *la linea* separating the two countries. Protected only by black shadows. My friend told me to look for a hole under the bars. I was so happy when I finally found the small hole. Like finding gold treasure. But I was way too big. I had to dig out more dirt around the sides in order to get my shoulders and my big *pansa* through. It was quiet. Dead quiet. The only sound was my digging

30

and panting. I only carried water. Good thing. I couldn't stop sweating. A mixture of desert heat and anxiety, I suppose. Hot. Sweaty. So hot. Around one-thirty in the morning I finally dragged myself to the other side. I remember in the distance, in front of me, a small light surrounded by pitch-blackness. The one the bartender told me to follow. A house. From there head east and cross over the dunes. *La Migra* was quiet. There was no patrol activity. Nothing else to see or hear. Only the occasional dog-bark echoing behind me from Los Algodones. Pitch-black. God awful hot. My shirt was soaking wet. Dirt and sand stuck to my sweat. I could hear my heart pounding inside my head. I remember. Pounding in a deafening darkness. My mouth felt like the desert. Sand over sand. Like a lizard. I kept reminding myself to crawl like a lizard. Fast and soundless until I got to the light. Crawling. My wedding ring strangling, my fingers pulsing. Keep crawling. Crawling on my full stomach. So uncomfortable. I thought I might throw up. I drank more water. Tried to push the acid down. I got close enough to the light to distinguish the shape of the house. *Ahhh, Dios!* I was relieved but still lightheaded and nauseated. Acid creeping up at the back of my throat. I ran out of water. My eyes burned like hell. I desperately looked for a faucet. I found one. Behind the house. I let warm water run over my neck and sweaty head. An old man opened the back door of the house. I didn't want to scare him. I whispered just loud enough to be noticed that I was drinking some water. He was kind. He asked me if I was okay and offered me a glass of cold water from the house. Drinking from the faucet was fine. I was still trying to catch up with my breath. I wondered how many late visitors the old man received. He smiled at me. Under the porch light I could see his eyes had a perplexed look. His aged and slow moving figure disappeared behind the back door. I turned my head back under the tepid water—dripping, panting and trying to catch an elusive second wind. My whole body was now

31

pounding. I could only hear the beating of a loud marching drum. I looked up to the stars and suddenly all was quiet.


Felipe Santos dressed in his spotless blue scrubs, escorts José and Eva Cruz through a maze of corridors and down flights of stairs until they arrive at a back room under the hospital's first floor. Eva's sweaty hands and slippery fingers entangled with her husband's start to annoy José. He tries to ignore his wife's nervousness. He maintains a cool and emotionless expression—a frozen moustache, a pure macho facade. Inside, just beneath his sun-beaten skin, he feels like a child wanting to cry. His life has hurt for so long.

The door leading to the room has no window, only a sign: *Restricted Area. Authorized Personnel Only.* Eva squeezes her husband's hand harder.

"Eva, there is no need for you to come in. You can wait here." José caresses her arm gently.

"No. I wanna see him."

Santos hands each a mask. The three of them, hiding their noses and mouths like authentic *bandidos,* enter the room. The door closes behind them with a distinct and lonely echo. They slowly walk towards the opposite corner of the room. Eva's eyes scan the tiled walls, bouncing from one empty place to another until they lock onto metallic legs of a table, partially hidden behind a white partitioning curtain. It's the only table inside the cold, hollow room.

On the table, covered by a white sheet, lies a body. The body of someone they know; someone who carried inside their shoe a single note with their phone number—no name, well-hidden, nothing else that could compromise someone; only José and Eva Cruz's phone number, in case something happened. Eva gasps placing her right hand over her mask. Her eyes, full to the top, are big and ready to overflow. She stands frozen behind José, still squeezing his hand and looking over his shoulder at the undisclosed body. Nobody makes a sound. Santos gives a nod towards José, who nods back in agreement. Like a ceremonial proclamation in slow motion, Santos pulls the thin sheet gently back exposing the lifeless, swollen face of the man.

José turns his head away and looks at his wife. Both, terrified and almost fainting, stare at each other to stay standing. José's knees wobble and he feels as though his whole body is going to crash and break into a million pieces right there on the white morgue floor. Eva hugs her husband and while staring at the body, her mind and heart instantly leave the room in shock. She imagines herself giving the news to Ernestina, attempting to comfort her dear friend with inconsolable and meaningless words. How could she explain to Ernestina the tragic fate of her husband's trip? Eva plays over in her mind the story told by Santos of the man crossing the border. She can almost see his big red face sweating. She can imagine his last few minutes and the old man from the house stepping outside again to check on the late night visitor; only to find the body of their friend lying in a puddle with an expression of suffocation, pain, and horror. *Ernestina must have known his heart was weak. She knew how much her husband liked to eat and drink.* Eva thinks about his family in Nayarit. His ancient parents, his brothers and sisters, all burying their son, their brother, in *absencia*. Not even Ernestina would be able to attend her husband's simple burial.

Time for me is meaningless. I watch Ernestina's loneliness. It burns me not to be there for her. I'm tired of this eternal wandering. I would give anything to be something: a dog, a cat, a butterfly to dart around Ernestina when she waters her roses; a worm, a cockroach—anything to be close to her. My only joy is watching her walk home from the market. Every day I watch her between fields covered with lettuce, spinach, and cabbage on one side and more of the same on the other. There, by the only tree in the middle of the valley, we spend our time together. The large branches and leaves paint a large shadow on the dirt. They give her shade from the long heated walk. She usually sits on a small rock and leans back against the tall tree. I wish I could be that tree, that Eucalyptus. Any part—the trunk, the roots, even a leaf. How I enjoy our private moments. As she closes her eyes, she always sighs deeply. I imagine she's thinking about me. I pray to be the rock she sits on. Sometimes, I become the tree trunk that supports her moist back or the faint breeze that touches her face. My queen has lost weight. Her dresses hang loose like the thin skin hanging over her bones. She's probably not eating enough. She's not taking care of herself. She works hard in the fields all morning then she runs home to receive the children after school. They all want her attention. They all want to tell her what they learned that day in school as though she were their mother.


Eva and José Cruz drive back from the hospital with painful silence lingering between them. Before José goes back to work in the fields, he accompanies Eva to the outskirts of Yuma to give Ernestina the news.

José waits for Eva under the porch by the front door of the house. The sound of children laughing makes José swallow harder. He stares at his wife not knowing what he would have done in his friend's shoes. Eva dries up her red eyes as she slowly walks towards Ernestina's door. Her heels sink in the sandy dirt.


There she is! She's coming towards me again. She's carrying two big bags full of groceries to feed *los niños*. There's no breeze. There's only the sun for lettuce, spinach, and cabbage to witness our encounter. This moment with her makes me feel so alive . . . Why is she stopping in the middle of the road? A white car? What the hell. Who are those two men in uniform getting out of the car? *Ay, Dios! No, por favorcito!* My poor Ernestina. No, she doesn't have any papers. Please, leave her alone! They want to take her to the house to find her papers. She has none. My queen is smart. She will never lead them to the children. Her house is a sanctuary on an unnamed dirt road.

Don't touch her! *La Migra* drives away with her sitting in the back seat. She's not scared. I can tell by her face. Her eyes, filled with tears, quickly glance at me . . . *mi mujer*, my love taken away and deported, the guardian angel for all those children.

Day after day, my Ernestina sits on the same bench as I did in the small plaza in Los Algodones waiting to cross. The hours of light, for her, are an eternal waiting for the hours of darkness . . . I'm here with you, *mi amor!* I scream and my words disappear like the fleeting chances Ernestina has to cross. Tomorrow night she will try again.

## Copenhagen
Jenny McBride

In Copenhagen they're deciding
whether or not to let Earth breathe
whether to keep churning her deep riches
into suffocation-wrapped junk food.
They're deciding again
if the world belongs to all or
only to a greedy few.

I have decided
I can live without facebook
but I really need my bike,
and that I don't need to fly again
so long as I can backpack in a wild place.
This has all been too easy
and I've got so much to spare.

In Copenhagen they're deciding
how many species will be left
when they cash in their writs of plunder.
They're deciding
how much a morning in spring matters.
They're deciding
why, even though you can't eat money,
it's the only thing of value to climate cannibals.

I have decided
to keep loving the snow with my skis.
I have decided
to really feel the journey of each migratory bird.

I have decided to hold the powerful accountable –
no insanity pleas apply.

## Kaleidoscope
Jenny McBride

When all the shifting,
the blur of falling,
the frenzied uncertainty
Come to rest
There's a beautiful pattern,
shape and color
fallen into
A perfect fit.
But while everything's moving,
when the present
has shattered
and familiar boundaries vanished
it's hard to believe
Everything will be smooth again.

# [the 25th letter]
Yuan Changming

yum yum yummy, you have
become so addicted
to this juicy alphabet
you can readily get high
high within your hairless skin
as yellowish as the bank
of the Huanghe River
less sleek than a china crane
but more fragrant than a young yucca
while its pronunciation can lead you
to the very truth you are pursuing, its shape
can grow from an unknown sprout
into a huge Yggdrasil, where your soul
can perch on an evergreen twig, cawing glaringly
towards the autumn setting sun

## The Day You Find Out Your Uncle Was Gunned Down by Police
Lis Anna-Langston

The day you find out your uncle was gunned down by police is a normal day. Normal as it gets. Thursday. Perhaps the day before you were thinking about throwback Thursday photos. Planning what to post. This one. That one. You were thinking about the dream where people kept telling you someone from the dead was trying to make contact. You were definitely thinking about that dream. Which is why you look your uncle up on the internet. With a cup of coffee in hand, no almond milk because you are lactose intolerant and too lazy to drive to Trader Joe's on Wednesday night. Remember, it is Thursday. The day you find out your uncle was gunned down by police.

It wasn't recent. The gunning down. That sucks. In the time passed you moved across the country. From the South to the North. To old battlefields and old wars. Old  buildings with bullet holes still lodged in the brick. You picked up coffee in the mornings and drove across the battlefields to the first place that felt like home as an adult. You left a way of life that dominated every breath for years. You left. You walked toward a future. You moved. You married. You moved again.

When you hadn't heard from your uncle in a while you sent emails. He loved emoticons and cute little chain emails. There was no response. That worried you enough to send a simple email. One question. Are you okay? No reply.

When you finally have a moment from unpacking and turning in projects and moving and marrying and new schools and jobs and cities, you log in and realize you haven't heard from him in a while.

A long while. He has children he loves. He doesn't need you to hover over his life micromanaging what he refers to as his senior moments.

But you are Southern and expect the worst so your internet search goes straight for the obituary. And there it is. His full name printed in the local paper where he lived. Lived. Past tense. In a single internet search his tense has changed. He's dead. There was a memorial. A funeral. A body. Suddenly he goes from being a person to being a body.

He was older. Almost seventy. It could have been of natural causes. Must have been natural causes. Which sucks. But {shrug} it happens. You do another search to find your cousin's address. You have three of them. You will send one a card. Your families have never been particularly close but you liked them a lot.

When you were little, around nine, your uncle moved to California. You saw him years later when he returned for a visit bringing an AT&T phone system that had a built-in answering machine, a speaker phone, and a hold button that played canned Muzak. It was the coolest fucking thing you'd ever seen.

Except he was rude. He believed you should obey regardless of the request. You threw some rocks at your mailbox and he told you to stop. Except they weren't his rocks or his mailbox and you resented him telling you what to do. So you waited until everyone was gone and filled the sink basin with his shaving cream. A huge, carefully formed mound of splendid, squishy foam. Then you washed it down the drain, as if to say, that is how fast I can get rid of you, answering machine or not.

## CONCLAVE

You didn't see him again until five years later. When your grandmother died. It was a mess. You were the only one who knew she was going to die because you'd been sneaking over to see her even though you were forbidden by your mother who was too high to actually enforce rules. So you weren't exactly in the habit of taking her bad advice. You'd seen your grandmother two weeks earlier and she couldn't get out of bed. You knew she was going to die. Knew she was going to do it on her own terms. And she did. No one ordered an autopsy. No one knows what killed her. No one ever will.

Your uncle arrived from California. Of the three uncles you started out with, you have two left. One disappeared years earlier. Went out to buy malt liquor and cheap cigarettes in an old flannel shirt and never came back. His truck was found on a Texas road, doors open, key in the ignition, engine idling, abandoned. Never seen again.

Now there are two.

You watch the adult family members fight over money. Your uncle is having sex with your mom's best friend. Which normally wouldn't generate much drama, except she's married. The absurdity of family makes you pray for it to all be settled and over.

Your uncle has a long history of not being able to deal with family and goes back to California.

You understand.

Even applaud him for his unwillingness to suffer through endless days of stupid.

Like stoopid.

The kind of stupid that is stoopid.
You don't know it then but when he boards that plane for California, that's the last time you will ever see him again in person.

With your own eyes. The year will be 1988.

But let's get back to Thursday. There's a stack of work to do on your desk.

And your uncle's obituary. Survived by children. Grandchildren.

And you try to find your cousin's address. What you find instead is a lawsuit filed by your three cousins against the city and the police department and having too many lawyers as friends you immediately know there is a summary and you scroll
  and scroll
and scroll

and read until your eyes and brain don't believe a word of what is typed on the page. For the first time all day you look away from the screen to a gray Pittsburgh morning unfolding outside the window. It is 10:34 AM. Your uncle is dead. He was killed by police serving a search warrant. You stand up. Get a cup of coffee. Drink some water. Stand in the kitchen. This is hard.

Realize that's why he never returned the emails. Realize there will never be any more emoticons. Realize you have no uncles left because the other one died in 2006 and your mother pretended he was still alive until 2009 so she could keep living in the house for free. Yeah, you're that kinda family.

Go back to your desk. Listen to the 911 call he made as the police entered his house. Go ahead. Lose yourself in that irony a moment. Calling the police to come save you from the police. Listen to his last words. It's not every day that a person's last words are preserved this way. The final minutes of his life play out. Realize that a TACT team came to his house to execute a search warrant. Go ahead. Luxuriate in that irony. Execute.

Your uncle was accused of having too many animals. All well-fed and taken care of. The news report says so. But the neighbors didn't like it. And they didn't like him. The 911 dispatcher was the final call he made. Not an I love you. Or an I'll be home soon. A desperate plea for help to a complete and total stranger.

Listen to him yell, "I ain't committed a crime. Get the fuck out of here! What are you bursting in my house for?"

All true. He hadn't committed a crime. Because technically having cats that are taken care of isn't a crime.

Unless you live in a white, affluent community that objects to you having your back door open so the cats can go outside. Say that again out loud. Leaving the back door open? No, the other part. White affluent community. Fancy way of saying your neighbors can get you killed without getting blood on their hands.

An officer yells for him to come out with his hands up. 27 seconds later they kill him. A TACT team to issue a search warrant? Shake your head. Your hands are shaking. This tactical unit is trained to respond to barricade situations, hostage rescues, counter-terrorism, and high-risk felony apprehensions and old white guys with too many cats. This is the exact thing your uncle railed about. People who give power to the police because they don't want to protect themselves.

You listen to him arguing with the police through a door. He sounds confused, almost childlike.

"Why are you breaking into my house?" he pleads.

You already know the answer. Supreme authority rules. And your rich, white neighbors want you dead because you are a nuisance.
You stop to think about why a TACT team waits until night to kick in the door of a 69-year-old man who was never officially charged with a crime. You see your cousin crying on the news. He looks so confused, so hurt. His daddy is dead. His daddy is dead. He loved his dad.

The internet is full of news reports. Pages of hits. Scroll. Scroll. It's so overwhelming. Who do you tell? How do you tell them?
Instant Message your husband. It's the only sane thing to do. After shock and a few minutes, a message flashes on the screen: The guy who killed him ran Homeland Security.

"What?" you say, absolutely incredulous.

Then you search the cop who killed him and the first hit is a LinkedIn profile. There he is, smiling big for the world to see. The man who murdered your uncle. We act like it's not murder if the cops do it.

But it is. Taking a life. A life taken.

A grandfather. A father. An uncle. A brother.

He wasn't a saint. You grapple with this fact. But he loved those animals. And he was proud of you. So proud of you.

Go back to the profile. Investigator at the police department. Homeland Security/Counter-terrorism. He specializes in high-risk entry. That's a fancy way of saying he'll throw a flash bang into a room and shoot you three times with an M4 rifle.
At close range. High Risk Entry. Mutha fucka.

The high-risk suspect begged 911 to send help. Who were they going to send? That part is kind of a joke, don't you think? No one was coming to help. Help was already there. Close your eyes and repeat that sentence until you believe it.

Your husband Instant Messages and says he just found out his stepfather was arrested for helping drug dealers launder money because he utilizes the same method for dealing with his family that you use. Total avoidance.

He learns his stepfather served six months prison time, then six months house arrest. He's a former jailbird turned snitch. Served on the County Board of Commissioners. He had to wear a wire. Government officials and career criminals are cut from the same cloth.

Then the riots break out in Baltimore.

Really. Because you cannot make this shit up.

You sit stunned into heightened awareness, watching anger on display. The media calls it "unrest." You snort and lean in close to the monitor like that hack reporter can hear you and whisper, "Burn that mutha fucka down. Burn it down."

It's a mantra. Repeated over the course of days. Burn it down. Not because you wish for people to lose their communities. Not because you don't think life is precious. You chant because the system is broken. Broken so far down the dirt is splintered. Bring that broken system to its knees. Bring it down. Bring it down to its broken, splintered parts and then crush them with your boot.

There's a guy in Baltimore dead. Your uncle is dead. Your husband's stepfather took a plea deal.

You write all of this down in a journal that you bought at the Louisa May Alcott house outside of Boston six months ago. You remember looking out at the ocean from the Boston shore. You think about when your uncle went back to Mississippi and found out his soon-to-be ex-wife wasn't taking care of the Arabian horses. Divorce was such a nasty word back then. God help us. Her name was Norma Jean.

You remember Boston. Remember the haunted inn where you had dinner. A quaint, charming New England town with squares and roundabouts. Think about how Mexico City is your favorite city in all the world. You're all ADD at this second. Someone has died. Someone is in the ground. You want to call your cousin. The one who told you that your grandmother never got a tombstone because your mom is an ex-junkie liar. Liar liar, pants on fire.

Focus.

The first time you were in Boston you talked to your uncle. Downtown near Chinatown. You saw a Mongol outside a noodle house. You bought a porcelain Buddha and thought about buying a tea set but how many fucking tea sets does one person need?

## CONCLAVE

Suddenly, you realize that all of your childhood photos were in your uncle's house. The ones your mother left in the garage. You realize they are gone now. Carted out with the contents of his life to the city dump. Humans bury everything. Nothing sacred. Nothing gained.

You remember throwing a pin from Paris off a bridge in North Carolina. Down into the river it went. You were afraid to bury your pain back then. Afraid if you buried it, it would grow. Had to let it go. Let it flow.

A staggering numbness claims your insides. Inside every cell. You can't shake it off. You stare at the hysterical commentators in Baltimore. Watch how a city in crisis is reduced to sound bites.
Take away the jobs. Take away the men. Take away the balance. Gun down everyone who is angry. Your uncle was a Libertarian. He was angry. Thought the government was a dangerous joke. Turns out, he was right.

There's his face. Right there in the newspaper. In a moment of dark-tinged snark you realize, like all good Southerners, you learn about what your family is up to on the evening news.

There's a curfew in Baltimore. Your uncle hated that marshal law crap.

You're pretty sure he killed a woman in Arizona and fled the state. You could never prove it. But you suspect it. He wasn't a saint.
Lay in bed with your husband and listen to the Baltimore police scanner. What a long three days. Long and hard. Death is supposed to be hard. Supposed to wrangle us out of ruts masquerading as comfort zones.

Look at the face of the man who gunned down your uncle. He's right there. He kills people for a living. Hard to get around that fact. License to kill. Your uncle is consistently referred to as a suspect in every news report. Yet he was never charged.

Lying in bed listening to the riots in Baltimore you are suddenly grateful that in the last years of your uncle's life you talked to him constantly for hours on the phone. Your cousin offered to take you to dinner. You got to know him more and more. He admitted that he loved junk and wasn't particularly tidy. That he wasn't the greatest about cleaning up but he loved his animals. He told you his neighbors hated him because he didn't want his lawn manicured and he didn't want to lease an Audi.

The news reports claim there were raccoons and opossums living in the house. It must have been those opossums that made it such a high-risk entry.

You wonder what ever happened to your grandmother's house. The one that languished into disrepair. You pull it up on Google Earth. There it is. Your childhood home. Emotion floods into your brain. You remember running up that front concrete walk a hundred million times. Maybe a hundred bazillion.

"That's where I grew up," you say to your husband, excited, pointing at the screen.

That was your childhood home. With your fingers you turn the view and travel that dead-end street two houses down where a Chinese artist lived. You remember the time you and your best friend went down and knocked on his door and asked if you could see the inside of his house.

CONCLAVE

He looked at both of you like you were off your rocker and asked
why.

"Because you're an artist," you said confidently because you were
sure you wanted to know what the den of an artist looked like.
Because he was awesome and good-natured and maybe even a little
flattered, he took you on a tour of his home while you ooohed and
aaaahed at every tiny thing, especially the fact that his home looked
lived in. He got paid for making art. Cash money. He was quite
possibly the coolest dude on planet Earth. His house is still there.
You have no idea what happened to him.

The National Guard rolls into Baltimore.

The last time you were in Baltimore was November, to see the
Snowden documentary Citizen Four. The problems didn't start in
one night. Everyone who loves Baltimore knows that. These riots
have been a long time coming.

You go downstairs. Sit quietly at your desk. Listen to the 911 call
three times. The last thing your uncle said in this world, in this life
is, "I don't know if you shot my animals or not." And his voice
quivers. And the tape goes dead. And so does he.

It's true he should have lived in Montana on a huge stretch of land.
So far out that he didn't have to see anyone. He didn't need the
superficial comfort of waving to neighbors or home delivery of mail.
He regarded humans as a lot not to be trusted.

That's how he came to live with cats, chickens, dogs, raccoons, and
opossums. There were no raccoons and opossums. The neighbors
made it up.

Your uncle rescued cats from the pound so they wouldn't be murdered in cold blood. He thought it was wrong. All that killing. So do you.

You could say his love of baby kitties got him killed. You could say it's about race but there is really only one color in the human race. Your true color. The news reports said the neighbors were saddened but relieved they no longer have to live next to him. He collected junk and put it in his backyard. He was a nuisance. Like a rat. His white neighbors are so relieved. After all, they got away with murder. Those zany white neighbors.

The man who gunned down your uncle has his own website.

His company's team is fluent in English, Spanish, and Hebrew.

He specializes in mitigating threats.

His birthday is December 28.

You can send him a request to connect.

# Stories from the Home Front
Ken Leland

A military band plays God Save the King, then glides smoothly into The Maple Leaf Forever. A steam locomotive filled with soldiers returning from the Great War rumbles into Union Station, where a thin line of city constables implores eager families to wait behind rope-linked stanchions. When the train shudders to a stop, hundreds of soldiers in khaki trench coats spill from a long line of passenger cars. Baggage compartment doors slide open and duffle bags are shifted onto a snowy concourse.

Straining, trying to look everywhere at once, I'm elated to see Richard descend almost in front of me. His long black hair has been cut short, and after four years overseas, he looks quite fit, but haggard too. I think he has grown a little taller. We're twenty-three now—surely it's time for him to stop sprouting up.

He drags his bag from the growing pile, drapes it over his shoulder and turns to scan the waiting mob. He waves and shouts "Maggie" when he sees me, and I let out a whoop, duck below the restraining rope and run to him. He lifts me in his arms to applause and scattered cheers from his mates, but I pay no attention. Eventually, I tear myself from his lips to demand, "Don't you ever leave me again!"

Front Street outside Union Station is jammed with shouting cabbies, double and triple parked at curbside. Seeking rides, families with uniformed sons and husbands climb over snowbanks into the street. Such confusion and noise are more than I can bear, but Richard raises his army cap and makes as if to wade into chaos.

I clutch his arm and pull him farther from the street, "All this, it's too much for me."

"But I can afford it," Richard says. "We got our last month's pay on the train."

"I took a room on Jarvis Street. Can you carry your bag that far?"

"Maggie, I need you something fierce."

"Let's run, darling."

Next morning at grey light, Richard insists we hire a cab for the short ride back to Union Station. At this hour, streets are almost empty, but even while he holds my hand, Richard watches storefronts intently. Grocers have begun to display their wares beneath canvas awnings; there are trucks and a few horse drawn wagons delivering vegetables, milk, bread and eggs.

"Maggie, this is how it used to be! No rubble, no artillery damage anywhere."

I smile patiently at him. "Darling, you're home."

He nods vacantly, turns to stare as we cross a slushy intersection at Yonge Street.

"There's one," he says of a labourer wearing a cloth mask that covers his mouth and nose. "And there's another. See Maggie, that woman over on Yonge is wearing a veil."

"What's it mean?"

"Spanish Influenza. It must be in the newspapers. Everyone in England wears a mask."

"Isn't flu just a bad cold?"

"This one kills."

It is mid December and the Grand Trunk freight takes us past grain and livestock farms, along rivers and lakes, edged with ice. The slow freight to Peterborough requires but a single passenger car to carry a few commercial travellers, a handful of timber workers, and us. Everyone clusters forward, near an iron stove, and I listen as Richard explains to them how with the Great War ended, the Empire's longest serving provincials are first to be furloughed home.

CONCLAVE

Silently I vow we'll never be parted again, that no call to duty will ever suffice to tear him from me. If need be, we'll live deep in forests for the rest of our lives.

By late afternoon we arrive in Peterborough, but it is another day's journey to Marmora, then north to Bonnechere Valley, to the village of Eganville. Single men sleep in a bunk-house at the train station; as a married couple, our tickets include a private room in a boarding house nearby.

After morning coffee, toast and jam, we return to Peterborough Station. Though Richard is a dear and very gentle, I'm starting to feel a little sore.

As coal shovels scrape, we board to continue our journey. After an hour's slow trek, roads and farms disappear and we pass into endless forests of birch, spruce and poplar. A night's snow and heavy frost have left only ponds of open blue water in the largest lakes. Pillows of white nestle on spruce boughs, tall birch are painted with snow, so delicately balanced even a breath of wind brings down cascades.

I dig into my satchel and pull out two woolen scarves I made, waiting for Richard's return. Both are patterned in red, black, yellow and white, and I stand before him. His brimmed army cap and trench coat are light brown, his deep black eyes sparkle as I wrap the scarves around his neck. I lean my head against his shoulder and close my eyes for only a while.

In early darkness, our train arrives at Eganville. Gently, I wake him. Here the Bonnechere River passes through a limestone canyon, carved to a depth of a dozen men standing on each other's shoulders. A little way upstream, a dam creates a wide lake and there are spillways for a lumber mill, a grist-mill and the woollen mill where I've worked since Richard was called up. The village spreads across both sides of this narrow valley, where east and west are joined by an iron bridge. Across the river, gas lights gleam in windows on the eastern hillside.

"I was worried we'd lose our cottage," I tell him as we step down onto a snow-covered, gravel street. "Mill wages barely keep me in food and firewood."

"Did you have to borrow? Wasn't my army pay enough?"

"We're free and clear, but only just."

"I'll find a job," Richard says. "Maybe the ice house will take me on, and there's always logging."

"You're the first man home from war."

Arm in arm, our way lighted by a waxing moon, we cross the empty bridge. Along its length are tracks of a single buggy in unmarked, ankle-deep snow. How odd, I think and pull Richard to the bridge railing to peer down towards factories beneath the span. At five o'clock, the work day has just ended, but I see no one.

"Where is everybody?" Richard asks as he brushes a powdered railing, watches snow swirl down towards silvery water.

Ahead, a dozen street lamps mark Bonnechere Avenue, but sidewalks are unshovelled, not a single person hurries home from work or shopping. No lights shine from Eganville's Town Hall, nor at the early-closed Emporium.

"Well, I didn't expect another brass band," Richard says, "but it looks like no one got out of bed this morning!"

"Darling, let's go home. We'll find our friends tomorrow."

We climb the eastern hillside, pass silent houses where single gaslights glow in parlour windows.

"I'm sorry," I tell him, "there's nothing fresh at home. I've been gone a week."

"Maggie, do you know what I'd like?"

"What, Darling?"

"Cornbread. Is there butter or jam?" he asks.

"Oh, yes! I left my jam crock with Bertie against a frost."

## CONCLAVE

"I'll fire the stove as soon as we get in."

From Riverview Drive, we turn east, uphill onto a dirt lane between the Anglican and Presbyterian Churches.

"Oh, Richard, you should have heard the celebration," I say. "When news came of an Armistice, boys rang church bells all day and half the night. School let out, there were bonfires and a sing-along at Town Hall."

He smiles. "Our battalion was camped outside Plymouth on rotation. A week earlier, we'd heard rumours of peace, and Methodist boys got down on their knees to pray we wouldn't have to go back to France. Maggie, I was down there with them."

"Of course you were. I was, too! Even man, woman and child across the whole world, praying it might be true."

Suddenly we are happy, so very happy the joy will last forever.

Our white-washed cottage with green trim is ahead, next to last on Mountain Lane.

I'm shaking, crying, as I try to slip my house key into the front door lock. Richard's hands rest patiently on my shoulders and he whispers, "Home at last."

"Maggie! Is that you?"

"Bertie?"

My neighbour's door is half-open to the night; candlelight leaks out onto her porch. Richard turns and begins to walk down our steps.

"Bertie Thomas, it's me," he says. "I'm home."

"Oh, Richard. Thank the Lord. I prayed so hard Maggie's man would come back alive. And you have!" Bertie retreats into her house, almost closes the door between them.

As Richard climbs our neighbour's steps, he calls, "Bertie, come out here and give us a hug. Where's Charlie?"

"Richard. Sweet Richard, don't you come no closer. We're both sick."

Now I can see Bertie holding a towel to her face.

"Charlie's like to die; don't know if I can last. You can't come in. Lord love you Richard, you dast not come in."

Why no. Of course, I'm not surprised what Richard does. I'm only a moment or two behind as both of us plunge inside to help.

Bertie, Charlie, Richard and I, and a hundred more that winter in Eganville, our graves lie atop the hill.

From here, it is a beautiful view, north to Golden Lake.

\*\*\*

On a busy summer sidewalk, I see them strolling towards me, elbows touching. I recognize her, it is Linda and a young man I take to be her husband. It's been four years since I left the north to study pharmacy at university. Though there is scant to show, I guess that Linda carries his child. As they approach, I stumble on smooth pavement, sidle from the path of city folk gathering for a midsummer's holiday. My head pounds and I lean against a shop window frame, struck dumb, helpless before her.

Linda's dress is modest, a print of tiny roses with a stiff, wide collar buttoned close at her throat, long sleeves ending in white cuffs, belt and purse of pale leather. Her dress stretches just below her knees to show bare legs and open-toed shoes. Curly brown hair frames her forehead and lovely eyes. Linda's nose was always a little too large, but she is no less precious to me. High cheekbones and determined chin, all features arranged in a pleasing oval.

God help me, why did I ever leave her?

She is close now, only a few holiday makers are passing between us. Attention averted to her husband, she senses something, perhaps my astonished gaze, and begins to turn towards the display window.

My heart stops when, with instant recognition, Linda's smile is replaced with shock.

"John!"

She darts out her hand to touch me, but pulls back.

"What's wrong?" her husband asks. He stops and turns to glare at me. "Did he try to grab your purse?"

Linda lowers her head, clutches his arm and firmly leads him onward.

"No, I mistook him for someone," I hear her say. "He's a stranger."

We're hardly strangers, I think. Over her shoulder, only once does Linda glance to me with yearning eyes.

Surprised, overjoyed that she has come to this place, I search the city, hoping that she does the same. On a rainy morning a week later, I see Linda queuing at a Dundas trolley stop. From across the street, my heart cries out to her and she looks up. Seeing my open umbrella, she mimes discomfort, turns up her raincoat collar.

As thunder growls, I hurry across to ask, "Would you share?"

"Oh, yes. Please."

She edges into the ring of falling droplets until her shoulder touches my chest. Arms crossed over her coat, she murmurs fiercely, "Damn you John. I waited so long, waited for you to come back to me."

"I was a fool," I say and glance at shop workers suffering wet misery alongside us. A streetcar squeals as it slows to take on passengers.

Masked by complaining brakes, she whispers, "I work till five at Eaton's, on Yonge Street."

As she sprints to board the crowded trolley, I call to her. "The southwest door."

Sipping from a tall glass of milk, picking at a slice of coconut cream pie, Linda smiles while I devour a roast chicken dinner.

"You have no one at home, I see."

Clatter in the busy automat mutes our conversation.

"No one," I tell her.

On the table between us, she pushes aside her pie plate. "Oh, John, I really shouldn't tease. Are you terribly angry I married someone else?"

"Of course not, it was my fault. I should have begged you to wait."

"Bill wanted to wed, almost from the day we met. You said it was over between us and it felt cruel to keep denying him."

"When I left for school, I thought to be unselfish, to set you free," I tell her. "But, my God, one look at you . . . what a mistake I've made."

She sits quietly, then reaches across to slip the fork from between my fingers, captures my hand in both of hers. She leans forward, stares into my face.

"This war is going to be worse than the last, isn't it?"

I nod. "Maybe a lot worse."

"I insisted Bill come south, get an orderly's job at Queen Street Sanitarium. I couldn't think of a safer place for him."

"A winter baby?" I ask.

"Yes, but Eaton's will sack me when I begin to show. It won't be long." Linda grips my hand tighter. "What will you do, John?"

"I'm a druggist. I might be drafted to a naval sickbay, or an army hospital somewhere."

"Don't be a sailor," she tells me with a sad smile. "You aren't meant for oceans."

I laugh. "I still can't swim."

She studies our hands. "Try to stay nearby. I'll need you."

59

## CONCLAVE

In the third week of September, leaves take on autumn hues. In Europe, two military powerhouses undertake dismemberment of a third country lying between them, and almost instantly, war is declared in all the Empire. A call to colours rings throughout our land.

While Bill is at work, Linda and I meet on Wednesday afternoons at Trinity Church. The minister who leads Bible study is curious about us, though we sit far apart among two score congregants. He can hardly fail to notice our eyes locking across the circle, that our questions and comments are those of kindred spirits, and today, my restiveness is unmistakable because Linda did not arrived before opening prayers. When, to my great relief, she does appear, she wears a dark veil and explains to all she mourns her father's death; her father, whom I know to have died seven years ago, long before I left for university. Still, her obscured face seems swollen.

Sitting beneath churchyard red maples, Linda tells me, "On Friday, Bill will quit his job at the Sanitarium to join up. He wants be a fighter pilot, or at least a flight mechanic."

I lift her veil and find bruises upon her cheeks. "And this is how he proves his valour?"

"I tried to convince him killing isn't an answer, to tell him it is harder to stand against war than to leap into its madness."

Linda hides her face from me and I seethe at the abuse. We clasp hands before her gently swelling belly.

From the church doorway, Trinity's minister looks out to see us huddled there. He approaches, speaking quietly, "Please, is there something I can do for you two?"

She shakes her head, takes my hand and stands quickly to lead me away.

He calls to me. "Help her, if she'll let you."

While we walk to her apartment, I'm filled with anger and uncertainty. Still, I know one thing, Linda has spent her last day with Bill.

As we approach on the street, I can see him leaning his forearms over a third floor balcony, a beer bottle held between his hands. He notices us, throws down the bottle and rushes back inside.

"He shouldn't be home yet. Please John, you have to leave, right now."

"Not a chance. You'll pack a suitcase and come away with me."

"You don't know him."

"I know what he's done to you."

Suddenly, Bill rushes outside the apartment building, onto the sidewalk carrying a baseball bat. Linda moves to stand between us, but I push her aside.

"So this coward won't fight? I'm not leaving you to him!"

With a chopping motion, Bill misses my head, but on the backswing, he drives the bat handle into my gut. Linda screams as I go down, winded. She bends towards me as he rears back again. His bat cracks against her skull and blood explodes. I crawl to shield her, but Bill swings at me once more, and this time he doesn't miss.

***

Hundreds of arrivals throng the city's Greyhound Station. Passengers, and those who would greet them, mill throughout the hanger-sized bus terminal, peering at flashing television monitors for late-arrival announcements.

As we step down from the Greyhound, two youngsters, who I guess to be in late teens, wave to attract our attention. "The Peace Resolution was defeated!" one calls out.

The young woman stands before us, crying. She carries a cardboard placard with 'Eileen & Robert' scrawled in crayon and the legend 'Society of Friends.' A young man is stalwart beside her, his head bowed as he reaches out to welcome us.

Robert hefts our backpack, glances at me and tells the weeping Quaker girl, "Eileen and I have heard nothing since Sunday morning. Border guards delayed us."

I shake my head and ask the youngsters, "So, no peace candidate can be nominated for President?"

"Peace Through Victory!" the young man croaks. "It's all the rage."

"Killing and dying will just go on then," I say.

The boy nods. "Yes, Eileen, that's what they want."

For lodging, they take us to a lakeside university, to a high-rise residence for married couples.

When I wake, Robert is standing in front of our bedroom window, naked to the world. Once I am able to tear my eyes from his bare legs and shoulders, I notice he's mostly concealed behind a white sheer. Early morning sunlight streams into our room, sparkles from a lake that extends south to the horizon. I flip the bedsheet aside to yawn and stretch. I'm hopeful he will notice and find his way back to me, but he is intent on a tourist guidebook in his hand. He leans past the curtain, looks out and seems to trace city streets far below, between here and the endless fields of parkland along the water.

"Eileen," Robert says, glancing towards me. "Come here, Darling."

It is only four steps from our bed to the window, but I sashay as best I'm able at this hour. I spoon my body against his back and wrap my arms around to caress his chest.

"Love, what's so important outside, for you to be over here, and me on the bed alone?" I kiss the nape of his neck, peek towards the guidebook.

"I've a riddle for you, Eileen."

"Yes?"

"Whose statue is in Grant Park?"

I laugh and tell him, "That's not how it goes." I smooth my palms over his belly. "The riddle is 'Who's buried in Grant's Tomb?'"

"Please, Eileen. Humour me."

"Oh, all right. Whose statue is in Grant Park? If it's not Ulysses S. Grant, I've no idea."

"Do you see that steep mound, maybe two hundred yards from the beach?"

I crane to one side but try to stay behind the drape. Upon a toboggan hill, there is an equestrian statue, the horse's neck arches downward, one hoof is raised; a bare-headed, Civil War rider clutches a furled flag as if to lead Union soldiers forward.

"Who is he?" I ask, moving my hands a bit lower to capture Robert's attention.

"General John A. Logan," Robert breathes as he turns to me with an ardent kiss. "The rally begins there at noon."

At midday, Robert and I wind our way to Grant Park where remote TV is already in position. "Look at her!" I hear one network cameraman say to another from their perch on top of a broadcasting truck. "Get a picture. That's one fine woman."

Promptly I stomp away from them, into the crowd gathering beside General Logan's hill, but soon I turn to see if I've lost Robert in the press. He's hurrying after, our smaller backpack bouncing on his shoulder.

With a broad smile, he says, "Why be angry, Eileen? That was simple truth."

"A truth for you to say," I tell him. "No one else."

Robert takes my hand and that helps me cool down.

We've been to so many demonstrations the last few years, some that became riots after murders or assassinations. We have learned preparedness.

## CONCLAVE

Robert is dressed unobtrusively in worn blue jeans and a long-sleeved, oxford shirt. His sideburns and mustache are common for men, but I can't endure a beard when we make love. Men seldom wear hats in summer, so at protests he is bare-headed, but he has taken to granny glasses now that we're in graduate school. Running shoes are *de regueur*, and in his shoulder pack are two water canteens, goggles, and large cotton bandages that double for breathing masks when moistened.

After seeing women pulled down and arrested, I braid and weave my hair tight—I would wear a pixie cut, but Robert always gets that lemon-tasting look. Runners and jeans, never a dress or capris, and of course, no cosmetics because of tear gas. Surely, I am very plain, drab even, although sometimes I get come-hither stares. When I do, I flash my gold band and hope they're smart enough to pay attention.

Half a dozen demonstrators have already climbed onto General Logan's horse and lead a growing chant.

"Peace. Now."

Late afternoon. Thousands have gathered, but the rally is running out of steam; rambling speeches and repetitive slogans will do that, even to the most dedicated.

Robert and I, and three score other couples, mostly Quakers, have staked our claim beneath a century-old, tulip tree. Lounging on shaded grass, we exchange news from Monthly Meetings, recount anti-war strategies, our successes and failures. The girl and her young man from the bus terminal are both here, other couples range from teens to middle aged, though a few are Elders. Plain speech and dress is passé, of another age, though for this occasion, Elders among us are dressed for easy identification, with frilled sun caps for Grandmothers, straw hats for Grandfathers.

General Logan is a quarter mile away across yellowed, August parkland. The dull throb of gasoline generators vies with bullhorns, making all unintelligible. Here at Grant Park, remote television crews suffer stupefying boredom. On a lark, newsmen bring shoulder mounted cameras to film our circle of Friends. One thrusts a microphone in Robert's face to ask, "Is this a love-in?"

I lift my head from Robert's chest that he might scan those around us.

"As far as I can tell, Sir, no one here is currently making love."

Nearby, teenagers snicker.

The reporter is perplexed but seems to join in the fun. "Later, eh?"

"Perhaps if you come back in a while."

The reporter hands his microphone to a cameraman, signals that filming should stop, then kneels beside Robert and me.

"Armed militia block all streets leading to the Convention. Thousands of city police will disperse this crowd at 6 P.M., after your permit expires. A protest march is forbidden."

The reporter looks up from Robert, raises his voice so those around us might hear. "It's going to be hell on wheels, in about an hour. Everyone, women at least, should slip away while you still can."

The young Quaker girl tells him straight out, "This is our fight, too."

Elders stand, pass word that we should remain here, then stalk away purposefully into the throng.

"The permit for this assembly has expired. This gathering is now illegal. Everyone will disperse, immediately. Anyone who remains will be arrested."

To the north a thick blue line, two thousand city police, bolstered by a second line of canine units, incensed German Shepherds, straining on metal chains. The first line of riot squads are helmeted and wear goggles; they are armed with pistols, mace and sturdy wooden clubs. In the east, the police line is anchored on lake beaches, in the west on an expressway. They will advance against protestors here on Logan's Hill. A similar force is already in position below the park and will press northward. Would-be marchers will be squeezed into deep water or onto the expressway if they would avoid arrest.

I see Quaker leaders returning now, accompanied by Mennonite, Brethren and Jehovah's Witnesses, ministers, priests and rabbis, all those who would make a Testimony for Peace this day. Elders link arms in the first row, men and women, side by side. Then another row, and another.

"Form up. Hold on to your neighbours. Don't let them fall."

Behind us are ten thousand more; young, old, black, white and brown.

Elders lead us west, towards the expressway.

Police rush to block the march but cannot. They attack protestors on the edges who suffer dogs, tear gas and flailing batons.

Demonstrators are beaten, bloodied, savaged before arrest.

Live TV cameras broadcast it all.

The young Quaker girl shouts a new slogan.

"The whole world is watching! The whole world is watching!"

***

It must not be supposed Eileen and I are harbingers of lost causes, though now all causes seem lost. And yet, hope still lives among a few.

Eileen is an old woman now, just as I am an old man, but if I choose to go into the city's streets today, I will find her there.

News of a demonstration has passed to us, in the now-usual ways. A covered mouth, a feigned cough as a subway train storms into a station; or on the street, lost in wails of passing security detachments: Noon Saturday at Government Park.

Spring 2016

We are no longer permitted to live together, but Eileen and I will be electronically observed, tracked separately from the moment we leave our domiciles until we meet at Government Park—association of criminals is a serious offense and we will be punished, along with everyone who dares assemble at noon. Identities of rally organizers and participants will be known to authorities after only moments of computer matching.

It is a price to be paid for peace.

# Digital Dust
Pattie Palmer-Baker

*The CIA hopes to improve its ability to trace the "digital dust" that potential targets leave during activities such as using an ATM card, renting a car, or moving through a city with a cellphone. Oregonian, March 6, 2015*

Tracking the target's unknown
the agent sifts digital dust,
not like stardust sprinkled
on profound black,
instead gray-brown specks
leaking out of ATM machines,
trickling from laptops,
dribbling out of phones.

He shapes the particles
into a digital fingerprint
blots out truth messy with color,
paints the grooves black and white.

Sometimes when the wind
blows through a Sitka Spruce,
he hears the whisper *As-salamu alaykum.*
He whips the gun
from the back of his waistband
and shoots the words
even though they mean
*peace be upon you.*

# The Sniper as Cupid
Shahe Mankerian

Mahabbah didn't know where to hide
when the sniper fired the first bullet.

Her satchel clinked full of breakables:
a jar of grape leaves, pomegranate paste,

a bottle of rose water. She squatted
behind a Mercedes sedan near the sidewalk.

Tony, the cabdriver, was inside.
When the sniper shattered the passenger

side mirror, he unlocked the door to get out.
But Mahabbah was there, bent over, trembling.

He knew to grab her and pull her in.
The sniper smashed the headlights.

Tony embraced Mahabbah. A bullet struck
the radiator. The hiss of steam veiled

the rapid heartbeats in the cab.

## A Letter From a Suicide Bomber
Olfa Philo

I'm the one who lives in the ghettos
a house with no secure roof
next to the garbage
cohabiting with flies &
struggling against floods
each winter...

I'm the one who was bound early
to abandon school
to work here and there
be responsible and care
for my infirm parents
and other burdens bear...


I'm the one who is born to live in the margin;
wear second-hand clothes,
eat  second-hand food,
be a second-hand citizen
with a second-hand identity card...

I'm the one whose sole pleasure is a cigarette & a beer
to inhale my pain and fear
evoke a casual  laughter
and hide the tear...


I'm the one who shouldn't even dare to dream
of females ... love...fusion...a nest...
for my heart was crucified long  ago

70

and this "luxury" I had to forgo…

I'm the one with no ambitions…no goals
for which to wake up, perspire or strive to achieve…
I somehow exist to survive not to live…

I'm not that handsome to be a Hollywood star
not that gifted to be a Maradona
not that smart to be a leader
not that insightful to fathom Islam
so ready for any Savior / Predator to be my mind-feeder…

I'm the one who feels alienated in his own homeland,
thus ready for relocation, exile or any flight to
Israel,
Syria,
Heaven,
Hell!
my soul to the DEVIL / DAECH,
I'm ready to sell…

I'm the one conceived in the State's womb
alas, my mother has never sensed my presence…
mistook her pregnancy for overweight;
did some sports…went on a diet…
yet once in labor with water, pangs and blood
could no longer keep quiet…
on her door, she felt the knock
no more time for her to turn back the clock…

too late for an abortion…

## CONCLAVE

too late for a miscarriage...
too late for an ultrasound scan...
my brethren fetuses will be soon born
and you have nothing left now
but martyrs to mourn...

## Before They Became Killers
Shahe Mankerian

What if Timothy McVeigh's fifth grade
teacher played Carl Orff on the turntable

while he practiced pirouette? What if
Eric Harris read The Very Lonely Firefly

in preschool and later created die-cut
collages like Eric Carle? At Virginia Tech,

Seung-Hui Cho enrolled in Nikki Giovanni's
poetry class. What if he never got kicked out?

What if he never wrote menacing poems;
instead, he memorized Carl Sandburg's

Fog by heart? And what if Syed Rizwan Farook,
on a field trip, visited the Art Institute of Chicago,

and on a whim, stood in front of Randall
Carl Bolton's screen print of Microbe?

## .400

Mike Koenig

I didn't want to be a sports writer; I certainly didn't want to cover the last-place Twins for an Internet site or live in a city like Minneapolis. I didn't even want to write about baseball. But that's what I found myself doing in the summer of 2015, several years removed from a torn MCL and the last lingering thoughts that I could play professional, if only European, basketball.

But something incredible happened to the Twins that summer. A third-year second baseman named Roger Murphy had caught lightning in a bottle. He opened the season with a thirty-game hitting streak and followed that up by hitting in sixteen of the next twenty. The Twins were sixteen games under five hundred by the All-Star break but Murphy was hitting .412, the highest average that late in the season since Rogers Hornsby. There was an energy in the stadium every time he came to the plate, a silent hush of expectation. He made singles feel like homeruns. And a three hit effort in a loss felt like a playoff win. Max Carlson, the old beat writer for the *Tribune*, turned to me after a five hit effort and said, "Appreciate this. It won't ever happen again."

I knew he was right; my blog could get ten thousand clicks if I simply typed the letters "H—I—T" in the title. But more than that, Murphy made me forget about my own athletic shortcomings. I loved the way he swung the bat. It was the smoothest, most natural, effortless, motion I'd ever seen. It was the way a three-year-old lets the wind blow bubbles from a plastic wand. When you looked at the swing it didn't seem threatening or powerful, but the bat always found the ball and placed it just beyond a fielder's reach. Watching Murphy made you understand what greatness was. And even if you knew in your head he couldn't keep it up, no one bats .400 for a season, in your heart he made you think anything was possible.

Most experts thought he would come back to Earth by mid-August. Baseball is a game of peaks and slumps: most .300 hitters aren't consistently .300. They bat .250 for awhile and .350 for awhile and over the season things average out. So while Murphy's hot start was impressive it wasn't taken too seriously by people in the know. Things get hot in August; hotter still when the national media makes you an everyday attraction. Not that I told Murphy any of this when he asked me to meet him for lunch following the All-Star game.

He was already seated when I arrived at the table, picking the onions out of a salad. I watched as he piled the small bits on a side plate.

"You can probably get a salad without onions," I said.

"You don't ask others to change just because you don't like something. If you don't like something you should fix it yourself."

I nodded as if I understood what he was saying, but truthfully I didn't think anyone would mind. I ordered a soup for myself and a soda with no ice, explaining to Murphy that ice hurt my teeth. Murphy didn't look up. He was eating his salad now one piece at a time. His eyes were intense, as if choosing which vegetable to eat next was an important, complex decision.

"Do you know why I asked you here?" Murphy was still looking at his plate.

"No," I said.

"I wanted to know if your website would be interested in writing a feature on me."

"Are you kidding? You're hitting .400; they'll give you fifty features."

"I don't want the article to be about my average. I want it to be about me."

"Like your life story?"

"Something like that," Murphy said.

"You're not on steroids, are you?"

"No," Murphy said with a laugh, "I assure you it's nothing as bad as that."

"I have to check with my editor, but I can probably get you on the front page Monday."

"Well, I don't want it printed until September. I think people will be following me more closely then. And this is going to be a big story."

"Big?" I repeated. "I'd love to write about you but if you want it to be big, you should go to ESPN or Fox Sports, hell, .400 could get you on Sixty Minutes. Sport Of Call doesn't have the same power as those guys."

"No," Murphy looked me in the eye for the first time, "I think you're the man for the job."

"Well, what's the angle?"

He put his hand on top of mine and passed his thumb over my knuckles. "I'm like you," he said.

I pulled my hand away. "I don't know what you're talking about."

We sat in silence for a few minutes staring at each other with a certain degree of unspoken truth. "If I'm still hitting .400 I want the story to come out," Murphy said. "If I'm not, we'll just leave it between us."


As I drove home I wondered what I had done to reveal myself. What I had said or not said to let Murphy know that we were the same. My whole life I had tried to keep things to myself. It was just better that way.

I was twelve when Magic Johnson announced he had HIV. I remember watching the *Arsenio Hall Show* when Magic went on a few weeks later. Arsenio, a product of the times, asked Magic if he was gay. When Magic said no a cheer went through the crowd like I've never heard before or since. The camera panned the audience and grown men, possibly strangers, gave each other hugs and high fives. The cheer lasted a few seconds but it was more vivid than the cheers from any of Magic's game-winning shots, louder even than the cheer for his skyhook that won the '87 championship. At the end of the interview Arsenio and Magic shared a long man-hug as if to say to the world that AIDS isn't so bad, and I cried because I knew that it was.

I wasn't gay that night. There were some boys I wanted to kiss and sometimes I thought about Michael J. Fox in a most non-Republican manner, but I had never done anything. And I knew as I sat alone in the basement of my parents' house, on their velvet couch piled with pillows and knitted throw blankets, that I would never act on these thoughts.

I wouldn't say I was in the closet in high school; but rather, in denial. I was sure that actions made you gay, not thoughts. So if I never went on a date, or looked at someone too long, if I never kissed a boy, then I'd never be gay. And since I lettered in basketball and baseball no one ever assumed anything different. In many ways I was the most homophobic kid on the baseball team, never slapping an ass or giving cup checks to an unexpecting friend, like so many of the other guys did. I was quick to call Sean McConnor a fag when he quit baseball to try out for the spring musical and always had a Playboy magazine, stolen from my father's collection, on the backseat of my car.

Sports were my sanctuary back then. When I was at home or at school it was just sex sex sex. But on the field it was what pitch should I throw? Is he expecting the change-up or the curveball? If he bunts do I field the ball or cover third base? No matter what the sport, there were a million things that could happen, and I was always thinking about what play would be correct. On weekends I spent hours going through hypothetical situations: men on second and third top of the ninth or, if basketball season, when do I shoot the three if we're down by four with sixteen seconds left. Saturdays were spent almost completely at the gym either shooting or throwing into a net; I'd lift weights or just run on the track, always supplying myself with game situations that might occur, constantly asking myself what to do if this happens or if that does.

But at some point I always went home and there was always that moment at night when I was alone in bed and teenage thoughts came to my head. Right before sleep I was always aware that if not officially gay I was also not completely straight. And as I masturbated myself to sleep there was never the image of a woman in my mind.


Murphy raised his average to .422 by mid-August. Even with a slump he would still be hitting .400 on September 1st so we agreed to meet for lunch a second time, this time at his house.

When I arrived he gave me a printout of "Hub Fans Bid Kid Adieu," the New Yorker piece about Ted Williams' last game.

"I'm looking for something like this," Murphy said.

"I'm no Updike," I said.

"It's okay. I'm no Williams." An odd statement since Williams was the last man to hit .400.

He brought me back to his office, which was filled with framed articles about his play in high school, nothing from the Twins or even his minor league career. He sat down at a red oak desk and offered me a soda, no ice. Then he just started to talk. He talked about his grandfather, who had helped raise him when his actual father ran off. His grandfather was a big Ted Williams fan who taught him everything about baseball, but also had strict feelings on what a man was supposed to be. He talked about how his mom caught him kissing a boy in eighth grade and told him the boy was fine but he was too young for kissing. "Just play sports 'til you're older," she said. He told me about the three men he had loved and had to break up with. One joined the army out of high school, the second had cheated on him, and the third just fizzled out around the time he was drafted. He was currently on a break from dating to focus on his baseball career but he was ready to start looking again, after the season. He was honest about his life. Like me he had never been harassed or bullied. In part because he didn't advertise being gay, but also because the type of suburbs we both grew up in weren't particularly outspoken about sexuality. There was just enough teasing to keep people quiet, but never any violence.

I took pages of notes that day, knowing his story and tastes as well as I knew my own. But always wondering what the endgame was. After three hours he took a break from speaking and reflected quietly on everything he had said. He looked almost surprised by his own forthrightness or maybe he was just surprised at how much he remembered.

"Are you sure you want to do this?" I asked.

"I think it's about time."

"No one knows I'm here. You don't have to out yourself. It's likely to cost you endorsements, money, maybe even your career."

"My rookie contract had a one-million-dollar signing bonus, a million dollars to play a children's game. I'm already overpaid and always will be."

"What about .400? It's been seventy years since anyone's done that. You want the pressure of that and the pressure of being gay at the same time? Why not just wait until the offseason, when they can't take it away from you?"

"My grandfather never actually saw Ted Williams play, but he talked about him like he had. He used to tell me that in '41 Ted Williams was sitting on .400 exactly. The coach said he could sit out the last day just to make sure he didn't ruin it, but Ted wanted to do it for real. He went six for eight in a double header to earn his .406. If I can't earn this as a gay man I don't want to do it at all."

"It wouldn't be cheating."

79

"Neither was sitting out the last two games." He took a long drink from his water glass. "Forget the history. I'm just ready. Aren't you ready for a gay All-Star?"

"I'm not the one you have to worry about."

"Everyone always says it's other people you have to worry about. I think we need to stop worrying about the few who may be upset. Most people don't care."

"Think so?" I asked. "Watch the kiss cam during the seventh inning stretch. See how often there are two men kissing. See what kind of applause that brings."

I never understood the idea of coming out. Especially if you were working in sports, where a certain degree of homophobia was, if not accepted, very much understood. I guess in a perfect world you could say and do anything. And truthfully I don't think too many people would care if I was gay. But if it cost me just one interview with a high-profile player it seems to make sense to stay quiet and not advertise something that has no chance of ever helping me.

Gary tried to convince me to come out in college. He was my first boyfriend, or maybe we were just lovers. He lived on my dorm floor freshman year; like me, he was gay without being obvious about it. I went to his room to watch a movie one weekend when his roommate had gone home. We were sitting on his bed as if it were a couch, our backs leaning against the wall. I had still never kissed a boy and the tension of a possible first time was excruciating. I started wondering what his penis was like, if I wanted it to be bigger than mine or if I wanted to be bigger than him. Not that I dared to touch his. In fact, I was using all my strength to make sure I didn't touch him at all. I just sat rigid with my back flat against the wall, my hands folded nicely in my lap. Every now and again we would look at each other; his face was stubbly and his hair messily covered his eyes. He didn't seem gay, and I didn't want to offend him by asking. So we sat in silence and put on a second movie, neither daring to make the first move that every molecule of air in the room told me we both wanted. Then the credits started to play but he didn't get up to turn off the movie. He just sat still. I turned to him and he grabbed the back of my head and pulled me into him.

It wasn't so much kissing as it was licking. His whiskers were scratching my face as we tried to angle our mouths together. Eventually we found a rhythm and a certain degree of sweetness. After a few minutes he took off his pants, I was happy that we were about the same size; no one would have to feel bad. But I made him wait. I wasn't ready to be full gay just yet.

I checked the peephole before leaving. His stubble had marked my chin and I didn't want to face any questions. I remember him saying, "let's not tell anyone about this," which was as good a plan as I'd ever heard.

But while I wanted the plan to last forever, Gary only wanted it to last for a few months. At Christmas he wanted to come out to his parents and wouldn't "stay hidden" from schoolmates during the spring semester.

"I'm not ready for that," I said, aware that being a college athlete meant being a guy.

"You really think it's that big a deal?" Gary asked.

"If it's not a big deal, then we don't have to tell people."

"That's not what I mean," Gary said.

"I don't know what you want from me."

"Bravery," he said.

"Being stupid isn't the same thing as being brave. This isn't anyone's business."

Gary never came back to school. His dad cut him off financially and he transferred to a community college. I said I was sad when he told me about it on the phone, but I was more relieved than anything else. The word Homo never had a positive spin on the basketball court so I didn't see much point in telling the team.

The funny thing about baseball is that some numbers mean a lot and some numbers mean nothing. A week after the story broke, Murphy broke the record for hits in a single season— 263. Literally doing something no one had ever done before, but the talk was always about .400, a batting average some twenty points off the all-time record and only six points better than Tony Gwynn in '94. In many ways, the achievement was randomly important— significant only because it was a round number. The number was like Murphy himself who was important not because he was gay, but because he was the rare male gay athlete. If he had been a pop star or an actor or a choreographer no one would have cared that he came out. But since he was a baseball player, an active player, it seemed that everyone cared and the more people cared the lower his average got. By September 15th he was down to .405 and with the great Yankees coming to town in search of a playoff spot, the valiant effort seemed all but over. He went 0-6 in the first game and 1-5 in the second. A pair of walks salvaged the third game but the 2-15 series dropped him below .400 for the first time since May.

Some reporters said he was getting pitched around and others blamed the umpires for changing the strike zone, making it hard for him to lay off pitches on the corners. But the truth was that the attention had changed Murphy. That easy swing was gone, replaced with something that resembled a fly swatter being used by an eighty-year-old man. I wished I hadn't written the story. I knew it was going to ruin his chances; I should have tried harder to reason with him, to explain the way the press works—that there are no parties for people who are different. But Murphy wouldn't have listened. Even as his average dropped he never pointed a finger; he merely said, like Ted Williams might, "baseball's a game of streaks, don't bet against me just yet."

Over the next week, he started playing like a kid. Bunting with no men on and running out infield singles. At times he missed the ball by four inches and other times he gently placed the ball out of a shortstop or second baseman's reach with the precision of a surgeon. It was far from the beautiful game he was playing in April and May but it was exciting. As the last week came, he was oscillating right around the magic number. Never falling below .395 or getting above .403. ESPN began breaking into the Twins games when he was at bat, instantly updating his average, and as the Twins came home for their last series, thirty-five games out of first place, it was generally agreed Murphy needed between seven and ten hits to make .400 for the season.

During the stretch run he called me almost every night. I was probably the only person he knew that wouldn't ask him questions about being gay or, worse, ask him about his batting average. We mostly talked movies during that last week. I kept recommending old Marx Brothers comedies that would keep his mind off the sport. But after going three for six on Friday night he brought up .400. "I'm gonna do it," he said, "I'm really gonna do it."

I laughed. His voice had both a sound of confidence and one of disbelief.

"Yeah, but next year can you make the playoffs so I can get some bonus money?"

Then there was a long pause on the phone, I wasn't sure if I had somehow insulted him or if he was still thinking about joining Ted Williams.

"Let me ask you something," I said.

"What's that?"

"How did you know I was gay?"

Murphy laughed. "What?"

"I never really thought I came off that way."

"Every straight reporter has looked at my junk in the shower. They never shy away from looking; they just want it over with. You always looked away, like you were worried about what people might think. That's when I suspected. Don't worry, none of the other players noticed. Your secret is safe with me."

And so it came down to the last day of the season. Murphy was hitting decimals points over .400. .400237 to be exact. But he refused to sit out. "Two for five," he had told me on the phone, "I just need to go two for five."

"You know it doesn't matter. I mean, you got the All-Star appearance and the hits record and the batting title. Whether you finish the season at .403 or .397 doesn't really matter, the difference isn't statistically significant."

"No," Murphy argued. "That's not true. Baseball has always been a sport of numbers. I got this attention because of .400. So I'm going to get my two hits. I want people to tell their grandchildren, 'Roger Murphy could hit with the pressure of the world on his back.'"

In the bottom of the first, Roger singled to left. But he struck out in the third and was robbed of a hit by a miraculous diving catch to end the fifth. He led off the eighth with a walk. Four pitches so far from the strike zone that the entire stadium started to boo. Barring a Twins rally, the walk would leave Murphy percentage points shy of the mark. But Sanders got a hit that moved Murphy to second, then there was an error on a Martinez bunt. Jenkins struck out, but Todd Mathers blasted a homerun to left that tied the game and guaranteed Murphy one more at-bat in the ninth.

So Murphy stepped to the plate with the bases empty and one out. The Tigers had retaken the lead in the top of the ninth, but no one in the stadium really cared about the final score. It was all about Murphy and history. The first pitch was about a mile outside and the stadium erupted in a chorus of boos. "Just give him a chance," I prayed. "Don't let the season end on two walks." Tonkin pitched the second ball into the dirt and I knew it was over. They were pitching around him. With a three run lead and no one on base they were pitching around history. Murphy swung at the third pitch, which was both high and outside. Then he screamed at the pitcher, "Not today." Tonkin smiled and nodded at the sign as he delivered the fourth pitch, again outside. But Murphy swung again and drove it to shallow left. It found the perfect spot between the shortstop and the outfield that epitomized Murphy's season. As he touched first base the scoreboard changed his average from .399 to ,400. He was so high from the achievement that he got picked off before the next batter saw a pitch. But as he jogged to the dugout there were only hugs and cheers.


I must admit I was wrong about the reaction to Murphy coming out. Most of the media supported him as a courageous and important figure. And none of his teammates seemed to care much about his sexuality. There were a couple of idiots who asked him if he looked at his teammates in the locker room and a few fans that held up some hateful signs. But the vast majority didn't seem to care that much and the big sports question at the end of the season wasn't should Murphy have come out, but rather should a player from a bad team be named MVP.

All in all I'd say more Americans supported Murphy during the final run and the deafening applause he was given for that final hit was the loudest I've ever heard a stadium get. So maybe I was wrong when I tried to tell him not to do the story. Maybe I was wrong when I thought it would hurt his career. Maybe hitting .400, being undeniably great, overshadows bigotry and ignorance. But I was right about one thing. There were no gay couples on the kiss cam during the seventh inning of that final game. No gay kisses with a gay athlete having a historic moment. I don't know what that says about the world at large, but I know it says something.

**Headed Toward Terra Incognita**
Louis Staeble

**Two Stories Down**
Louis Staeble

# Utopia
Jeremy Schnee

News that we found Utopia excited the entire world. Everyone asked how such a place had existed without notice by explorers or scientists, how such a place had not been seen by planes or satellites. There were explanations. Our main concern after revealing the discovery was that everyone wanted to go to Utopia, and such a perfect place wasn't meant to be visited by just anyone.

The name wasn't actually Utopia. We, popular media, preferred this term as more befitting. The company originally had sent our small team to map iron deposits near the North Pole. Anomalies with compasses turned us every which way. Hence, one reason Utopia wasn't found previously was that the planet's magnetic field dips over the coordinates. Lucky for us, we ran out of gas and set out on foot for survival. We could have as easily died. Snow and ice served like fortress walls. Stumbling through this maze, hypothermic and on the brink of collapse, many of us later admitted we thought we had passed over. One minute we walked in sterile white, the next, every color of the rainbow bombarded us.

Utopia gets sunlight all year. The sky over the place is bluish— with patches of aqua and strands of purple. The region is smaller than a moderate airport. As ice melted from our faces, we practically tasted the zest of the fruit adorning all the trees. Smooth slate paths offered welcome balance for our tired legs.

The place could not exist without a perfect coalition of circumstances. Rock encloses the ravine and underground minerals absorb geothermal heat. Even the cove has glistening sand, foaming waves, and lush sea-life when just a stretch beyond, icebergs collide. The mix of temperature extremes create vital haze—a bubble barrier that conceals the place and refracts sunlight, star glow, and aurora lights to provide circadian day/night cycles. The haze holds warmth like a blanket and even turns falling snow to mild rain.

CONCLAVE

Amazing as our initial shock was at finding tropics in the Arctic, we then saw the people.

We called them Shambahlans, Edenites, Alfheimers. They were a skin-tone somewhere between the outer shell of a coconut and inner pulp of a nectarine. Diversity in hair, eyes, and facial features suggested a mix of all world peoples. None were overweight and the men seemed tall, the women curvy. They wore togas and cloaks. Their response was not hostile, yet our need for a rifle and flare guns seemed necessary considering our surprise. They smiled, some waved.

Not expecting them to understand our language, we extended a greeting. They muttered nonsense and called someone out from what we later learned was a library. He began to nod in acknowledgement as if our language was something he studied long ago. He began to speak, translating for others who spoke simple and single words. Our first question was naturally to ask where they came from. They pointed away and said they also, came from outside.

They were a colony. Of what time and place, they were uncertain. They did not write history down like us. Houses, paths, and bridges suggested Utopia was both old, and, though difficult to explain, new. The society did not operate the same as most. For starters, Utopians did not have jobs. They had pursuits. A Utopian may decide to update a path. Stone by stone, they'd polish and reset the entire thing. They may build a perfect house, even if not intending to live in it. Others may decide to make clothes for the populace. People were paid in encouragement and gratitude.

To us, the concept sounded like a recipe for laziness. Pictures that captivated world attention however, came from such pursuits. The famous stone fountain up the ravine, with water in reverse gravity, was a result of one man's pursuit. Sun-spot seven, the sitting place between prisms that speeds healing, came from generations of pursuit. The toy that tapped magnetism of the cove so young Utopians could glide with wings was a recent development by a woman allowed a century to think of it. Trees and plants were cultivated over seasons and bore foods we never imagined. Books were truly one of a kind.

Infrastructure was both function and expression. Streams of snowmelt provided running water. No pipe, canal, or aqueduct worked in the same way. Houses were unique: some wood, some stone, some in, or on, trees. One house had a roof with curtains of food growing down. Room remained in the environment for bugs and animals. Hummingbirds were especially cherished. Old space was allowed time to overgrow so future generations might create on blank slates.

Nothing truly compared to the people, though. Beautiful, yes, and we were surprised to learn they had no words for things like adultery or crime. Utopians sought single mates, yet no documentation officialized this. Laws weren't written. Perhaps centurions—who we mistook for elders in their sixties—recalled instances when someone got an idea to step out of line. If so, the community decided how to handle them. The abundance of food helped to keep peace. We can attest to dipping nets in the cove and pulling them out heavy with sea life. Trees and gardens belonged to all people. With no option to expand into surrounding cold, they kept the population stable.

One problem with pictures of Utopians was the inevitable urge of lust. Our group had a similar problem in person, but then we noticed something innocent and naïve about genuine love between man and woman. Seeing close families helped make leaving Utopia possible—we missed our own.

The company had a conundrum on our return. Utopia sat on vast deposits of invaluable minerals. We showed pictures, explained that though less advanced technologically, narrow-minded of the wider world, something special existed in Utopia. We spoke of food, the cove, of the art and culture. Many company executives wanted to visit. Thus we saved the place and added a new and valuable company asset: tourism.

Besides, the company could hardly bulldoze Utopia with all the world watching. Reporters interviewed those of us who found it. We appeared in magazines and on TV. The company promoted us to curators. Someone had to preserve the quality of Utopia. Artists and hippies saw the place as a haven. Religious leaders claimed a divine right to spread word there. Scientists wanted it untainted, yet also wanted to visit for study. The whole world seemed to see Utopia as a drop of clarity to purify their bucket of mud. Other nations even tried to say Utopia should get divided and parceled out. The company stayed a step ahead, using influence to ensure stewardship. The company also held the best resources to transport visitors across the treacherous landscape.

Good-natured Utopians greeted our clients with open arms and tables of food. They talked into the night and shared their homes. After some months, however, the size of feasts declined. The community needed debate on where to put visitors. The company helped by importing food. Utopians were thus introduced to convenient mixes and shelf-stable foods. They rejoiced in trying junk food. As for imposing on their homes, the company did the considerate thing and built a hotel.

Not in town, the hotel lay hidden outside the haze. Our guests still had to adorn full dress to get through snow, so we built a tunnel. The glass door in the ravine did ruin the guests' otherwise perfect pictures of the place. We provided photo-editing service. The door also created security issues. Some of the aforementioned hippies, artists, and scientists attempted to sneak into town by getting menial hotel jobs. The company stationed guards.

The Utopian elders around this time expressed some alarm, claiming we were all in danger of losing the good place. To the elder's disadvantage, their community made decisions as a group. Offers of further convenience swayed residents our way. Easier than extracting squid ink, we passed out pens. We gave lighters for stoves, offered options people never considered over discipline and care: birth control. Utopian kids with too eclectic skills in fishing, furniture making, weaving, and stargazing, took quick to the allure of modern gadgets. Our hotel catered to youthful Utopian interest in TV and music. The company later offered the young a chance to travel, attend college, or take a helicopter ride and see something aside from a town surely feeling small to those with many long years ahead. Generosity from the company was part of a strategy only later admitted to those of us in charge. Wealthy guests had around this time begun making momentous offers to acquire vacation homes in Utopia.

A few impetuous youths sold out first. The company's commissions from such sales, our bonuses, were impressive also. Never mind that homes were traditionally given by the community and meant to return to it someday. The wealthy newcomers ushered in new amenities. Electricity, after all, could benefit everyone. The company next offered an alternative to Utopians who strained over what to pursue. They offered focus—needing people to manage generators and power lines. The company could not rely on whims of pursuits and appointed specific Utopians to construction and repair positions. They even hired hosts to ensure all guests received satisfactory cordiality. Those who saw such repetitive work unappealing quickly became the next round of Utopians to sell their homes.

From here on, events which led to catastrophe in Utopia became rather gray. First, the company offered access to modern medicine and insurances to protect from disaster—something far more tangible than the communal net elders put faith in. The company instituted education standards, and later helped create and pass concrete laws. Technology became common. Utopians were given citizenship, even official voting rights. Those of us originally appointed curators of Utopia did not see these changes firsthand.

Bonuses from home sales had allowed for early retirement. Yes, we were guilty of greed, but we were also as helpless as if a museum owner sells off great sculptures. Our group had also grown disillusioned with company choices. So we turned away. A few years later, the only intrigue about returning to work was chance once more to visit that fantastic place. We were naïve enough to think the company catastrophe unbelievable when they called for our help. They claimed Utopia had disappeared.

We arrived at the hotel to see the haze bubble. We followed the tunnel toward adorned paths. Our joy ceased the moment we set foot inside. Gone was unique architecture, replaced by modernized homes. Gone were hanging ornaments of fruit—trees starved in shadows of homes that expanded upward. Gone were hummingbirds, poisoned by fertilizers that kept plants lush. Gone was that aura of color once dancing on haze—eaten away by radiant electricity. The company even sold art bit by bit when home sales revenue declined. The waters of the cove receded when dams created more beach space.

Not a single word of the old language was uttered. The library displayed works suitable for new citizens. Paths underfoot appeared more like a random kaleidoscope than yearning expression. Laughter did not float from children above. The gliding toys had been bought by a private investor to be rented out; eventually wearing down, with no one left knowing how to fix them. Company-paid employees shuffled about, cleaning and welcoming us. The staff admitted to being non-native. These employees simply eked out an existence, hoping for crumbs to fall from the banquet of money. With ritzy shops, overpriced coffee and food, we may as well have been archaeologists expecting an ancient wonder and instead finding an amusement park.

The company inquiry never led to conclusive answers. The company actually became too entwined in lawsuits with those same wealthy who had purchased homes in Utopia. They claimed the company put on a ruse to falsify value of the place. Those of us who had found Utopia vanished into obscurity, fearing we face similar fate.

We never did have time to answer the most important question of all: where went the Utopians? We found none in our search. Company records indicated frequent turnover of homes before the catastrophe. Not a single Utopian that once attended college, or left suggesting they'd start a business elsewhere, was found in our wider world. Even looking for art, books, and inventions resulted in dead ends.

The chance is likely Utopians acculturated perfectly to our world and collectors stowed artifacts away. We had another theory. Utopians were clever, perhaps craftier than expected. Might they as we first invaded their world, have planned to infiltrate ours? We had expected squandering and laziness after making them wealthy. These were not their typical traits.

Implausible as it seemed, maybe Utopian people reacquired their art and artifacts. The world as they learned, was large enough to perhaps have a few hiding spots left. If they put their minds to it, pursued such a thing, we imagined they could go about anywhere. This was a nice thought; it kept the company searching. For those of us who had seen the town untainted, the only thing we felt sure of was that given chance again to "discover" Utopia, we wouldn't.

Much of the rest of the world seemed in need of imagining where it might be, how and when it might turn up. If Utopia was found once after all, surely, could it not be found someday again?

# Kali Must Dance

Susheela Menon

*Kali—the Hindu Goddess of change—stands marginalized in Indian homes as we turn towards less expressive female deities. Why are we afraid of our most radical Goddess? It is time her spirit rises to strengthen a country that has overlooked horrific cases of gender violence -- one of the most obvious challenges it faces today.*

There is something about the Goddess with the sickle and skulls. She exudes something not many women in my family exhibit: unbridled rage.

Her dark face—expressive, feisty and powerful—rouses an intense emotional response that's both intimidating and inspiring. She wasn't part of the family of deities that graced our little bedroom in Mumbai, but the child in me sought her startling form as I wandered behind my devout parents, who seemed almost oblivious to her mystical presence.

The rest of the Gods appear too benign but for Shiva, Kali's consort, who wears a serpent around his neck and sports a vertical third eye that promises endless destruction. No force instills in me as great a wonder as Kali, who slays demons without mercy and sticks her bloodied tongue out at all of us.

No one talks much about this deviant incarnation of Shakti—the female force in Hinduism. She is a mysterious spirit that could strike you down or drive you insane if you annoy her. Her persona has built an impenetrable fortress around her through which few humans want to venture. I can't tell what lies behind those flaming eyes except that they have an angst in them that's rarely seen in mankind today.

96

I have seen her pictures hidden away in remote sanctums of temples or in desolate corners of villages that pray to her. Mother tells me that none worships the aggressive form of Kali in their homes. Why, I ask. Mother doesn't know. Docile and silent, Mother holds a wellspring of strength within her, but it never shows. Father sounds and looks more forceful though even as a child, I knew Mother was the stronger of the two. Mother lacks something Kali has in abundance–expression.

Kali is a radical power—unconventional, unafraid and unapologetic. She beheads her oppressors and dances atop their dead bodies. She drinks the blood of the fiends she slaughters and is as unrestrained as she is fearless. She inspires rebellion and reaction through the sheer force of her presence. Her skin is the colour of the night and her fiery tongue sticks out at us, expressing blatant contempt. The garland of skulls around Kali's neck, her long, black hair, firm bosom, and hideous tongue are all ideas that contradict each other. How can a woman so beautiful be so brutal?

Self-expression is what defines this magical Goddess and there is something about her that intimidates Indian society. I wonder if her assertiveness is what makes us uncomfortable. The sight of a woman gone wild doesn't appeal to everyone. Deities are role models and Kali's fiery tongue and flashing eyes may not be what you want to see in your progeny, girls especially. Many spiritual masters believe she is a force that was crystallized or created by mystics aeons ago. She can come alive but unless one needs her energy for a purpose, it's best not to venture into her space. Her forms are many but as I sift through the hundreds of myths and metaphors that surround her unusual disposition, everything looks obscure.

Researchers dispute the origins of Kali, with some saying she was a pre-Aryan Goddess and others claiming she may have been a tribal warrior. Her name is derived from the Sanskrit word for Time, which has led many to think that she symbolizes Time. As Time destroys and devours everything in its wake, so does Kali, the great destroyer. Kali is also a Hindi word meaning "black," and thus her name perhaps signifies nothing but her dark blue or black skin. She is associated with tantrism, black magic and sorcery, and is known to live in cemeteries where the dead lurk. Though several stories swirl around her dark existence, she remains a shadowy Goddess.

It is difficult to weave together the many time periods and texts that influence the way we worship our deities, but it is easy to see that cultural variations have a huge role to play in the philosophies of religions. Early Hinduism saw both men and women as equal, depicting Shiva (matter) and Shakti (energy) as unable to exist without the other. Shiva did not possess Shakti. She had her own identity but together, they stood as one and ultimately belonged to the sole truth—Brahman.

Shaktism, a denomination of Hinduism, has its roots burrowing as deep as the Upper Paleolithic period (approximately 20,000 B.C.E). As societies evolved, Shaktas, who believed in the supremacy of the feminine force and revered powerful female deities, found themselves facing a decidedly patriarchal set of beliefs that accepted feminine deities but in subordinate roles. As patriarchy tightened its grip on cultures, women stopped being significant in Hinduism. The identities of the Mother Goddesses worshipped by early Shaktas later merged with the characteristics of Puranic Goddesses like Parvati and Kali. They became consorts of powerful male deities and were less fierce than Shakta Goddesses who defied subjugation in any form. Stories from this era hint at clashes between male-worshipping and female-worshipping cults, which often led to patriarchal temples denying fierce Goddesses the right to enter by terming them evil or destructive. The existence of Shakti in Hinduism is a direct denial of patriarchy but Kali's stormy form and vicious temperament have kept her away from mainstream Shakti worship in Hindu homes. Kali–the ugraroopi (fearful)–is looked upon with great trepidation. We are uneasy about Kali because she is almost feral in the way she exhibits her emotion. As a people, we are not comfortable with fearless display of sexuality or wrath. Our grief is as muted as our love sometimes.

There are only a few places of worship scattered across eastern India that celebrate the ferocity of Kali, the most popular among them being Kolkata's Kalighat. Kerala–my native land—worships her as Bhagawathy, the divine Mother.

Built in the 1900s and surrounded by Gods and Goddesses of all temperaments, our ancestral house had a spot dedicated to Bhagawathy where ceremonial worship and animal sacrifice were practiced annually. The holy Mother's nightly meanderings around our house kept thieves and demons at bay. I was terrified to know that Grandmother could hear the sound of her anklets every night. "Hear that? Chillu Chillu," she would say, "Our Bhagawathy protects us from the formless demons that sit atop these palm trees." It was strangely reassuring to hear that a Goddess watched over us. It was also a little unnerving to know that there were formless demons that could fly down from palm trees.

I am yet to see the murderous form of Bhadra Kali in Chottanikkara near Cochin, where exorcists work hard every night as the possessed struggle to rid themselves of spirits with the help of the fierce deity. The mentally ill find solace at Chottanikkara by driving nails into a Devil Tree with their bloodied foreheads under the Goddess's steady gaze. The annual festival of Bharani at Kodungallur

Bhagawathy temple—also in Kerala—sees animal sacrifices, oracles and bawdy language being used to appease Kali and her devils, thus branding her a demonic energy or a destructive force lusting for blood.

The thing about myths, Father says, is that you can't prove it right or wrong. You either believe in it or you don't. We have cast our Gods in our own image, and are more comfortable with women who know how to hide their angst and their sexuality. Kali's existence as a destructive female force is the most disturbing form of Shakti as it rebels against convention. Her stories are shared with caution that limits questioning. Don't question myths, warns a friend. His fear strengthens my curiosity. I decide to explore more. It is tough to translate the actual meanings of the many fables that religious texts hold within them but I wonder if there could have been an attempt at trivialising the power of this dominating Goddess by distorting her history. As stories travelled across generations, did these myths conform to the culture of the times that they were uttered in? It is up to us to form our own interpretations, Father says.

Various myths warn against the untamed dance of Vama Kali (the terrible form), which could signal an end to the world we know. Her wrath can wipe out the earth. She appears to be at the zenith of power as she is seen straddling Shiva, even eating his entrails, in a painting that could be centuries old. What left me wonderstruck was the way in which Kali's sexuality was depicted. Her ferocious mating with Shiva signifies much more than what the mind can interpret. Is it Kali's brazen sexuality we are afraid of or her refusal to be the subordinate? Or is it both?

It is not possible to erase Kali from our midst as she manifests all beings. She is the Supreme Mother. She exists not just in sanctums but also deep within our individual and collective psyche. I have seen her appear several times in women who have revolted, rebelled and dared to do things differently. Stories have been weaved around them just as myths were circulated about this avant-garde Goddess centuries ago. From young girls who question tradition to women who openly defy patriarchy—Kali delights in rebellion, assertion and expression. Many have challenged her resurgence but the regularity and vehemence with which she emerges is enough to tell us that India will bow down to its women soon.

I ask Father about the demons that could have inhabited Kali's land during the times that these myths were written. Who were they and where did they come from? Father doesn't know. Mother mutters that they are still around. Yes, they still exist. As a woman, Mother knows this.

How else do we understand men who gang up to rape toddlers? What do we call those who smell sex in a child who is yet to leave her dolls behind? They are modern day demons and their destruction demands much more than new laws and attitudinal change. One of my male friends recently pointed out that we almost always ignore male rapes. I agree that men too are at the receiving end of abuse sometimes, but would it be factually incorrect to say that regardless of who the victim is, the perpetrator has almost always been the male?

It is this standard that Kali breaks, as she is never the victim. Our stories speak of meek women who are silent regardless of what they have to endure. Kali grabs tradition by the scruff and turns it on its head as she defies any conventional definition of a woman. She rules every narrative that exists about her but lies dormant within mankind today. It is her silence that has strengthened the evil around us.

As girls, we were conditioned to live with anger that never found any expression. It never occurred to those around us to file reports or pressurise local leaders to highlight public safety—especially the safety of women and girls—as top priority in their manifestos. None stopped gangs of goons from commenting on the bodies of women who walked past them. They then grew to touch, grope and molest as people around us looked away. We shuffled around to escape those hungry hands, mortified but silent. Women who resist are now being thrown off trains and buses. Their defiance has triggered a spate of acid attacks that have disfigured and maimed some for life. Our collective silence led to atrocities as ghastly as the one Jyoti Singh—one of India's bravest daughters—suffered in December 2012, but our state didn't measure up to the anguish that the women of our country displayed at the time. Instead of seizing the bull by its horns when public wrath was at its highest, it let the matter slide yet again into the dark spaces of our minds. We are struck by the many divisions we have created within us—of caste, class, religion and gender—and we seldom unite to reach a consensus or build pressure on the state. There is a lot of outrage at Gods being offended or holy texts being burnt, but few care to act if children as young as two are abducted and gang-raped.

The viciousness with which Singh was assaulted opened our eyes to a new kind of savagery. It wasn't about lust anymore. This was hatred in its vilest form—a seething, frightening hatred for women. The term misogyny was heard many times during the months that followed the attack. Every possible factor, from sexual repression to sensitisation, was discussed to death. Social activists have repeatedly reminded us that abuse is rampant within the four walls of a home too. Danger lurks in the form of a father, brother or uncle, not just a stranger on the street. And yet, how many times have we heard our leaders talk about a definite roadmap to curb such violence? It is absurd how a society so steeped in female worship can be so blasé about female infanticides, gang rapes and dowry deaths. We move around like hermit crabs, hiding behind shells that sometimes can't accommodate our bloated conscience. We have become an impassive lot and are afraid of anything that challenges our apathy.

Jyoti Singh has been erased from public memory by the many things that define the chaos that is India, but her parents continue to nudge societal conscience by actively seeking a lot more in terms of justice and change. She was flown to Singapore, her body in tatters, by a government rattled by large-scale protests against its inability to protect its women. Left to perish with a friend on the streets of New Delhi, Singh stirred a revolution that threatened the political party in power at the time. She struggled to live and told us her story. Her testimony led to the arrest of the five men who had nearly ripped her apart and her death stands as a glaring example of how deep-rooted hatred is for female expression in many parts of India. She held extraordinary strength that exhorted her to stay alive despite having suffered beyond human endurance. The Goddess lives—in all of us.

I write this as the nine-day festival of the Hindus comes to a close. We have burnt effigies of Ravan and chanted the Devi Sthothram. We have danced the Garba and cooked feasts for young girls to honour the Goddess in them. A few of us worshipped the Kali of the cemeteries on Naraka Chaturdashi, the day on which the Goddess slayed Narakasur, a demon from hell. Some of us were told it is Lord Krishna, not Kali, who killed Narakasur. We went back then to our texts and tales to check on truths and fallacies, ignoring the many Narakasurs that have risen since the slaying of the one from hell. We allowed the demon to return but robbed Kali of her rage.

## CONCLAVE

As believers of karma, we think everything happens for a reason. The violence we see around us must be for a reason too. Could it be to shake us off our collective stupor, to help us find expression?

I do not sense Kali's dark, wild presence in any home yet but I know that she has started swaying. Her legs throb with intense excitement and her eyes narrow in anger. It's a matter of time before she begins her frightening dance, her garland of skulls beating against her bosom. Her tongue awaits the blood of the demons she intends to behead and her eyes flash with fury, as she gets ready for the long battle ahead. I listen to the sound of her anklets. Her manic laughter mocks our cowardice. She stopped dancing centuries ago but the fire in her will not let her rest for long.

Kali lives and will dance again. She will find expression in the thousands of girls growing up in different parts of the country and reclaim her place as one of the most inspiring Goddesses in the Hindu pantheon. We must keep her alive for we need her fire. Kali must dance her dance of domination, passion and indomitable strength. She must dance. And she will.

**I Love You Laura**
Louis Staeble

## Urban Girl & The Pending Blood
Siaara Freeman

at sixteen, my father was murdered, i learned
the difference between saying goodbye and wanting
to say goodbye is
  a bullet,

is a close call that finally gets close enough to leave
more than stories. & yet still leaves nothing
more than stories.
   & a woman who melts back into girl
   & looks for love again & tries to forget
    the crime scene her daughters face reminds her of.
   & a daughter who spends a great deal of time trying to become
the one who got away. who spends a great deal of time deciding
that she'd rather be empty & needing
to be filled, than to be full & needing
to be emptied.

i learned forever in the hood don't mean the same thing it does
everywhere else. here it means pending. Pending: incarceration
Pending: my untimely execution Pending: anything
i don't have complete control over.
forever in the hood pulls like a band aid. it hurts & it's over
before you
know it.
  pulls harsh & confusing like the wrong end
of a lit cigar.

## Urban Girl Catches a Glance Of Herself in the Mirror Before Stripping
Siaara Freeman

I too told them the idea of so much clothing was absurd
I too told them my body was a power
a wedge of Africa they could never tame
You too look like Atlantis
the wand that chooses the hand that holds it
The girl who walks into the sea and swallows
her own
name.
You look so familiar woman
what child were you yesterday?

**Steadfast Like a Rock**
Daniel Wu

**What's Over the Cliff**
Daniel Wu

**Entrance to the Sky**
Daniel Wu

# Near-Death Experience
Dallas Woodburn

William had a stroke. A mild one, the doctor said. But he was out for a few minutes. I found him in the living room, collapsed beside my bag of knitting, his cheek against the carpet, the television blaring Larry King. The window was open; from outside came the rumbling of a truck, the laughter of the children next door playing in their front yard. It had been a midsummer day breathless with heat, and the stifling heaviness lingered into the evening air.

Of course I was scared when I saw William like that. Of course my heart started beating fast and I ran over to my husband and stroked his face and tried to wake him. Of course I called 9-1-1 and cried into the phone for an ambulance.

Later, when I sat beside William's hospital bed and he reached over and squeezed my hand and smiled, I felt relief like none I'd ever felt before. I wasn't alone in this world. He hadn't left me yet.

But then he came home from the hospital, and he started going on and on about God and Jesus and being "saved" and "seeing the light." At first I thought it was just a phase, just something he had to get out of his system. But it's been four months now, and if anything he's just getting more belligerent about it. He wants me to go to church with him. He wants the two of us to get baptized together. He keeps a Bible on the nightstand and reads passages out loud before bed, like a preacher in a movie. I always roll over and pretend to be asleep. Any response from me would just encourage him, make him dig in his heels even more. William is stubborn as the waves crashing onto the beach, breaking rocks down into sand.

"Did you pray for me?" William asks.

We're sitting at the breakfast table, sunlight peeping in through the thin yellow curtains. It's the first week of October. Overnight, it seems, the summer warmth has been wiped from the air. I'm taking a gardening class at the community college—*Eat Your Own Home-Grown Vegetables This Winter!* the course listing promised, which made me think of the Laura Ingalls Wilder books my mother read to me as a girl—and when I signed up for the course it was my mother I thought of. She's been dead for years, yet still I find myself ranking my actions on her scale of approval or disapproval.

Today, a Saturday, I will plant my vegetables. I'm drinking ginger tea and eating warm toast with jam and thinking about my new trowel and sunhat and the feel of moist soil between my fingers. And then William has to ruin the moment with his talking.

"When I was in the ambulance?" he persists. "Did you pray for me?"

I sip my tea and stare at the curtains, trying to glimpse images in the folds of the cloth and the patterns of light shining through. There's a maple tree right outside the kitchen window, in the side yard, and its branches cast shadows onto the sunlit yellow. William planted that tree shortly after we moved into this house, more than twenty years ago. We were newlyweds then. We put a lot of effort into sprucing up this place—painting things, planting things, buying things. Trying to make this house ours. Trying to turn it into a home.

I remember how strong William seemed then. He is not a tall man, but he has broad shoulders and back then he stood very straight, his chin lifted up a little when he talked, which made him seem taller than he was. Sometimes, when he hugged me close, he gripped me so tight it hurt. To be honest, I liked the helplessness he brought out in me. It was what drew me to him from the beginning. It was what made me marry him. The belief he would take care of me, yes. That he would provide a good life for me and for our future children. But more than a promise of security, I think I was attracted to a recklessness I sensed in William, a hint of danger in his strength—the knowledge that, if he wanted to, he could pick me up and carry me off somewhere, anywhere he pleased, and there was nothing I could do about it.

After he planted that maple tree outside our kitchen window, William was jubilant. It was just a sapling, with small leaves poking out tentatively from thin branches, but William was taken with the idea of it. "This will grow into the tallest tree on the block," he said, kissing me, his hands leaving smudges of dirt on my face. "Just wait and see. Someday our kids will climb this tree. I'll build a tree house for them to play in. How's that sound?"

"Wonderful," I said, pressing my cheek against his, kissing his neck. Back then, I wanted a houseful of children. I thought children were like geese and we would have a gaggle of them.

"Sarah?" William says, bringing me back to the present. He places his hand on the table, beside my cup. He could reach over, just so, and graze my wrist with his index finger. If he wanted to. But he hasn't touched me since his stroke.

"Did you pray for me?" he asks, a new urgency in his voice.

I could get up and walk out of the room. Walk right past him into the living room, upstairs to the bedroom, and close the door. I could walk around the kitchen table and out the sliding glass door and into the garden, pulling my housecoat around my waist against the dewy morning chill. I could stay right where I am and reach for the newspaper, unfold it slowly, study the smudgy print, and act like I don't hear him. Ignore him and ignore him and ignore him no matter how many times he asks.

But I don't do any of these things. I tilt my face up to meet William's grey-green eyes, filled with a new earnestness. I ask, "What do you mean by pray?"

When William was taken away in the ambulance, of course I thought, *Please let him be okay*. Words ran through my brain like charms. *Oh Dear God Oh Dear God*. Words crammed my brain, the same words over and over, squeezing out all other thought until I was left silently chanting: *Please please please please please*. Sitting

113

alone in the corner of a hospital waiting room, fingers rubbing back and forth over the rubbery waxen leaf of a fake plant on the magazine table, waiting for the doctor to come back and tell me something. *Pleasep Leasepl Easeple Aseplease.* I want to ask William, Did you know that when you say a word too many times, its edges begin to bleed together until it loses all meaning?

Is that what praying is?

"Did you ask God to save me?" William asks, scooting his chair closer to mine. "When I was taken away in the ambulance, did you ask Him to grant me more time here on Earth with you?"

The absurdity of hearing this type of language come out of William's mouth causes my body to tighten, as if shielding itself from impending hurt. My hands clench around my mug of tea. I can hear it in William's voice—he's not saying him, he's saying Him. Upper case. *Did you ask Him to save me?* I want to say, "Okay, you can stop the act. You got me good. But that's enough, all right? Enough now."

Instead, I laugh. I can't help it.

William frowns at me, then pushes his chair back and leaves the room.


I started taking classes at the community college after I learned I could not have children. To ease the gnawing emptiness of my womb, I took up pottery, basket-weaving, knitting, quilting. I stuffed myself with facts about World War II, the French Revolution, Imperialist Japan; I studied French for two semesters, imagining a trip to Paris with William, walking arm-in-arm along the boulevards and sampling wine in the sidewalk cafes. But then William lost his job for drinking too much at the office holiday party and kissing the boss's wife. I was not there. The dental office where I worked had its own holiday party that night, and I was hanging up garlands of fake pine when I got the phone call from William asking if I could come pick him up. In the weeks following—the marriage counseling, the Alcoholics Anonymous meetings, the tears and accusations, the night I threw a wine glass and cut William's forehead so deep he needed stitches—I stopped going to French class and threw away the Paris brochures I'd bought. The make-up sex made me feel like I was hurtling towards life and death in one simultaneous dizzying blur.

The only person I told about William's indiscretion was Marlene, a fellow Midwest transplant who I met Photography 101; we've taken a class together every semester since. She did not mince words. "Sarah, listen to me," she said. "He's never gonna change."

But William needed me. He told me nearly every day and it was exhilarating to hear, like the catch I heard in his breath when I climbed on top of him and held his wrists against the bed, knowing in that moment I was the only one who could give him what he wanted. He was trying to sober up—very hard, he was trying—but he would never be able to do it without me there. He said this and I knew I could not leave him.

When I get home from work, William's sitting on the couch— sitting very close on the couch—beside Alice Townsend from two doors down. They seem deep in conversation, but both look up when they see me come in.

"Sarah!" William says, as if I've been gone three weeks.

"Hi, Sarah," Alice says, scooting ever-so-slightly away from William. "I just stopped by to see how you two are getting along." She's a russet-haired young mother of twin boys. Her legs are longer than a flamingo's and she's wearing shorts. She's the only mother I know who can get away with wearing shorts. "I'm so glad this guy is doing okay." She pats William's knee, once.

CONCLAVE

There was a time that coming home to a scene like this would have made me intensely jealous. Worries about William leaving me would flit around my mind constantly, keeping me awake at night, making me jittery and forgetful during the day so I'd get people's appointments mixed up and double-booked. Eventually I would collapse into tears, and William would get frustrated and tired of "talking in circles about the same damn thing." He'd storm out and come home drunk and I'd wake up to his large hands on my thighs, his lips kissing my neck, his breath warm and insistent with apology. Afterwards, I'd nestle into him and we'd both sleep like the babies we'd never have. In the morning, my worries would start up again.

But that was years ago. Now, he's telling Alice Townsend about the instant before his stroke, when—"for no reason I can explain," he says, "it wasn't a commercial or anything"—he glanced away from Larry King on the TV and felt his eyes drawn towards my bag of knitting on the floor beside his favorite armchair. A royal blue ball of yarn was poised at the top of the bag, for a sweater I'm knitting for Marlene, whose favorite color is blue and whose birthday is next month. In the weave and fray of the ball of yarn, in the shadows playing across its surface from the glowing side table lamp, in that instant before his stroke William swears he saw the face of Jesus.

"And I thought, *Jesus, you are my savior and I love you,*" William says, taking Alice's hands in his own and gazing her full in the face. "And I felt this warmth through my entire body." He pauses for even more dramatic effect. "And I knew, right then, that everything was going to be all right."

He lets out a big breath of air, and so does Alice, and I watch them smiling at each other. Alice wipes away a tear from the corner of her eye. Ever since William came home from the hospital, when I've witnessed moments like this between my husband and someone else, I want to be different. I want to be someone like Alice. Someone who can share that with William—a feeling of awe, giddiness, triumph at his salvation. But I don't believe that Jesus really appeared before my husband in a ball of yarn in my knitting bag. I've pretended a lot of things the past twenty-three years, but I can't pretend to feel that.

Last summer, before William's stroke, Marlene and I signed up for a poetry course and read Yeats' poem "Leda and the Swan." It made me think of William. *Her thighs caressed/By the dark webs, her nape caught in his bill/He holds her helpless breast upon his breast.* Our teacher spoke about the classical myth the poem was based upon, where the Greek god Zeus takes the form of a swan and seduces Leda.

"This isn't seduction," Marlene said, holding up her photocopied handout of the poem. "This is rape. The swan is raping Leda."

To my surprise, the teacher agreed. The entire class agreed. I nodded along, because I didn't know what else to do. I wasn't about to raise my hand and ask, *Am I the only one who thinks this is a sexy poem? That maybe the swan loves Leda, loves her so much he can't stand to be without her?*

On my first date with William, he ordered beer after beer all through dinner—he must have downed five brimming pint glasses by the time we were finished with our meal. I don't remember what I ordered or what we talked about. Mostly I remember the dark brown walls, the glass-topped tables, the way the pint glasses left rings of moisture, a mosaic of wet smeary circles. I remember the way William grinned at me, winking as he said to the waitress, "Yeah, I suppose I'll have one more." And the waitress would come back with another foamy glass, not batting an eye, calmly refilling my iced tea as she set the beer down in front of William.

The thing about William was, he did not seem inebriated. He did not slur his words or speak too loudly or tell off-color jokes. He was charming and fun and he looked me as if he had been waiting his entire life to bask in the glory of my presence. He said I looked beautiful. I was wearing a red dress with a sweetheart neckline and a wide purple belt I'd found at a thrift store. I thought William was unspeakably handsome. I thought it was sophisticated and manly, the way he was able to hold down all that liquor without seeming drunk. I was twenty-two years old, new in town, infatuated with the beach and the sunshine and the freedom of living halfway across the country from everything I'd grown up knowing. I had a part-time job as a secretary at a small dental office. Nights and weekends, I painted cartoonish landscapes of cornfields and farmhouses in fluorescent colors. I gathered sand from the beach and mixed it into my paint for texture; I decorated my bedroom with seashells and driftwood. I saw myself as a daring artist living the grand *boheme* life.

But I was lonely. My only friends were Suzette, the 52-year-old dental hygienist who worked afternoons at the office, and a girl named Jo-Ann who had been sorority sisters with my high school friend Charlene's cousin, and who I occasionally met for coffee before work even though we didn't have much to say to each other than analyzing what had happened on *Dynasty* that week. My typical Friday evenings, before William leaned in through the glass partition separating me from the dental office waiting room and asked if I was free for dinner sometime, usually consisted of peanut-butter-and-banana sandwiches, halfhearted pencil sketches in my notebook, and falling asleep to Johnny Carson. After three weeks of dinners and drinks, when I finally caved in and slept with William for the first time—on a blanket in the sand dunes at midnight, ocean waves murmuring on the edges of my consciousness—I was sure I would never see him again.

But William surprised me. He kept calling and coming around, and within a year he asked me to marry him. At our wedding reception, he was a little over the edge of tipsy into drunk. No one else seemed to mind, or perhaps they didn't notice. Even sober,

William was one of those loud, flamboyant guys who liked to be the center of attention. His flushed cheeks and crazed dance moves could very well have been the uncorked energy of a happy groom about to embark on his honeymoon. But I knew William, and I could tell he was drunk. When we slow-danced together, he pinched my bottom and kissed my ear wetly, sloppily. His breath smelled of bourbon. "I love you," he said, and it made my heart sink because I loved him, too, and deep down I knew in a vague, bleary way that perhaps William needing to binge on alcohol meant that something in his life was missing. That something between us was missing. But these thoughts happened in a place of my brain that was easy to push away and ignore. And so I did. For years and years, I did.

*How can those terrified vague fingers push / The feathered glory from her loosening thighs? / And how can body, laid in that white rush / But feel the strange heart beating where it lies?*

That day last summer, I arrived home from poetry class, opened the front door and called a hello to William. There was no answer. I found him unconscious in the living room, the television blaring Larry King, the laughter of Alice Townsend's children floating in through the open window.

Ever since his stroke, William has not touched a drop of liquor. He has not sipped a single beer. He hasn't even thrown them out— the cans remain in our fridge, couched between the jar of mayonnaise and pudding cups and carton of milk. The whiskey and gin and rum bottles glisten in the cabinet beside the stove. It is as if William relishes the temptation—the knowledge that he is living purely in a house full of sin. Or perhaps he is so confident in this new salvation he has found, this new self he is trying on, that he does not even feel tempted.

Since I will not go to church with him, William invites some of his church friends over for dinner. He asks me to make spaghetti. "Your famous spaghetti," he says. "Everyone loves your famous spaghetti."

According to William, my mother made the best spaghetti sauce he ever tasted. The trick, she said, was a pinch of sugar, to cut the acidity of the tomatoes. My spaghetti came in second—"a distant second," he once said, after a few glasses of wine. He must have seen the hurt on my face, because he immediately tried to take it back. "I'm kidding!" he shouted, grabbing my arm as I turned away from the table and tried to stand up. He pulled me down into his lap. "I'm only kidding," he said again, taking a sloppy bite of spaghetti off his fork, sauce flecking his face with red. He wiped his cheek against mine, and his whiskers grated like sandpaper. "You take everything too seriously," he said.

"Sorry," I said. Somehow I was always the one apologizing. If you had asked me, I wouldn't have been able to articulate what I was apologizing for.

I agree to make spaghetti for William's new friends. As I dump the box of brittle noodles into the boiling water, I think of my mother in her hot kitchen in the summertime, rolling out thin strands of pasta dough on the cool marble slab she kept beside the sink. She spent hours in that kitchen. She said she enjoyed cooking for her family. Mostly, though, I think she was cooking for my father, trying to impress him, or at least please him. My father, with his thick gray mustache and unsmiling eyes, never said one nice thing about my mother's cooking. Or, if he did, I never heard it. After she died, he threw away all her cooking supplies, married a blonde twice-divorced D-cup named Linda, and moved to Florida like a tired cliché.

Tonight, I've no need for a pinch of sugar. I don't have the energy. And I don't care what these church people think of my cooking. I take another pot down from its hook above the stove, pop open a jar of Prego, and pour.

They arrive bearing sparkling cider and wide smiles: Rick and Suzanne, Jim and Peggy. Before his stroke, William was never much of a hugger, but now I watch him hug each person before ushering them inside. His new friends. His people.

I place the cider on the table, along with a bottle of white wine. Jim and Peggy exchange a look.

Suzanne leans close, her hand on my arm. "You must be so proud of Liam," she says.

*Liam?* William's grandfather was Irish, but he's never wanted to go by anything but William. He doesn't even like me to call him Will.

"How long has it been now?" Jim asks.

"Almost six months," William says, beaming. "And you know what? I don't even miss it."

"That's wonderful, honey." I try to make my smile natural. "You know I'm proud of you." And I am. How long have I wished and wished for William to drink less? How many nights have I worried about him driving home? Still, I can't help but feel insulted. Cast aside. I've spent every year of our marriage trying everything I can think of to help him sober up, and nothing has ever worked for long. Now all of a sudden he's "found the light" and he's quit cold turkey, just like that?

Rick and Suzanne, Jim and Peggy—how are these people enough for him when I have never been enough?

Without looking at William, I pick up the bottle of wine. It feels damp under my fingers, moisture beading in the warmth of the room. The bottle is full, heavy. A weapon. I tilt the lip against my glass and pour.

"Cheers!" I toast the room. "You don't mind, do you, William?"

"Of course not," he says. I search for tension in his eyes, his smile, the set of his jaw, but he looks relaxed, happy. Peaceful.

Over dinner, Jim tells a story about when he and Peggy went to Israel and Peggy took a trip to Bethlehem by herself. "I was in meetings all day," Jim says. I seem to have missed what his meetings were about, but he's ploughing on, talking about how dangerous Bethlehem is these days, especially for Americans and women. I pour myself another glass of wine. Jim smiles at Peggy like she is a puppy that stole a sock from the dryer. "I knew my girl would be all right," he says. "I knew it was something she had to do."

Peggy nods. "It's the Holy City," she says. "I had to go there. I had to."

"You know, I wasn't even worried," Jim says. "Because I knew someone up there was looking after her and He wouldn't let any harm come to my girl."

Everyone around the table is smiling, but I feel anger rising within me, a warm steady burning. I take another sip of wine. *See, this is what I don't like about you people*, I want to say. *You're so sure God is looking after you—that you can do reckless, senseless things and still be safe from harm.*

I take another sip of wine. A big sip, more like a gulp.

*Everyone who dies—it's like you're saying that God wasn't watching over them, that he doesn't care about them. Don't you see how damn self-righteous you're being?*

"Sarah, please!" William says, his face pained. Everyone is looking at me with round surprised eyes and I realize with a sharp ache that I've said this last part out loud.

It's all William's fault. These are not my people. This house does not feel like mine with them here. This can't be the same dining room William and I painted all those years ago, newlyweds with a big can of barn-red paint, carefully maneuvering our brushes along the baseboards and crown molding in the corners.

How did I get here? How did we get here?

"I'm—excuse me for a minute," I say, stumbling out of my chair, standing up and pushing it back into place. "I'll just be upstairs. William, there's cobbler on the counter and ice cream in the fridge for dessert. I mean the freezer—there's ice cream in the freezer." And I flee.

There's something I've never told anyone, not even William. When I gave birth to Hannah, I died. I left my body and felt myself hovering over everything. I looked down at the small bright room, at my own body in the hospital bed, at the ring of doctors and nurses surrounding me with their charts and instruments, at William, pacing along the back wall, alarm evident on his face— and, despite all the signs to the contrary, I felt an overwhelming sense of peace. I knew, with more conviction than I've had about anything before or since, that everything would be all right. Hannah would be okay. I would be okay. He, up there, was watching over us.

The next thing I knew, I was waking up in a different hospital room. William was sitting on a chair beside my bed, looking out the window. I said his name and he turned to me, and I saw it right there on his face.

In that moment, I stopped believing in God.

What I want to tell William—what I want to tell everyone downstairs, throat-clearing their way through peach cobbler and coffee—is what I know to be true. Salvation is smoke and mirrors, a comforter we wrap around ourselves and hug close to keep from going crazy. Because if there was a God, he would not have let it happen the way it did. Not only losing Hannah, but not being able to have any children, ever? Nothing to hang on to, nothing to hope for, nothing to even begin to fill the emptiness? I couldn't paint anymore. Anytime I tried, I would end up staring at the blank canvas for hours. I burned the last painting I had been working on—

a calm, moonlit ocean for Hannah's baby room—and threw the rest of my paints and supplies away.

"The world is a cruel place," I say softly. And then, because it feels good, I say it again louder, almost shouting. For a few moments I wait for the rhythm of William's footsteps on the stairs, coming to soothe or reprimand, but the low murmur of voices from downstairs is uninterrupted.

Head pounding, I lie down on top of the bed William and I share, on top of the quilt I sewed in that maw of grief that was my life after losing Hannah. The quilt is made out of scraps from my maternity shirts and William's blue jeans. I sewed the entire thing by hand because I couldn't bear the noise of the sewing machine.

Lying on top of the covers makes me feel raw and exposed. Even in the summertime, I lie underneath a sheet. In the early years of our marriage, William and I would sleep naked, curled against each other, skin warming bare skin. Now, I unhook my bra and turn on my side. A bobby pin digs into my scalp but I don't have the energy to remove it.

Later tonight, William will wave goodbye to our guests from the front porch. He will rinse the dishes and put them in the dishwasher. He will spoon the leftover pasta into a plastic container, and the sauce into its own separate container, and when I open the fridge in the morning to get milk for my coffee the two containers will be there, stacked neatly on top of one another. He will step gently, quietly, upstairs and look in on me, sleeping. My mouth will most likely be open, snoring drool onto the pillowcase. William will unfold a blanket and drape it over me. I will not wake up. I am a heavy sleeper, especially with the wine. He will sleep on the couch downstairs, waking up early because tomorrow is Sunday, and he goes to the 8 a.m. sermon and then out to breakfast with his church friends.

I want to open my eyes in the middle of the night and feel his body curled around mine. He once held me for three days, rocking back and forth in this great big bed as I cried and stared emptily at the walls.

On our first date, William drove me home. Looking back, I am sure he was too drunk to drive, but that night I wasn't worried. He opened the car door for me and I climbed inside without a second thought. I was twenty-two years old, wearing a red dress with a sweetheart neckline, on my first date with a man who looked into my eyes as if he was searching for salvation and I was the only one in the world who could give it to him. He drove with the windows down and radio turned low. Everywhere was the sound of the ocean. If his car veered to one side of the road and then the other, I didn't notice. He may have driven too fast, but I didn't care. The air against my face was cool and smelled of salt. I closed my eyes and thought, *Thank you*. I was willing to go wherever he would take me. I was sure we would make it there safe, together. I was sure it would be somewhere nice.

## Resharpening the Interim
Rikki Santer

Pencils should be better
privileged, their gift
of starting over.

So many working titles—
some of us envy others,
others don't mind

on the sly,
on the run,
most ache to trust

tenderness, lust for
more days insatiable
with nomnomnom color.

To speed up that feedback
loop for more toys to hitch
to a star, logrolling so fast

in our own cartoons.
But it's all in pencil
as we compress towards

the gray horizon. Slow
down from the rewind—
sketch the last face

that will say I love you,
your last day to erase
the slate clean.

**Visual Art**
Eleanor Leonne Bennett

# Three Miles to Agnes
Elaine Gallant

I know these roads. They fan down the hill in a gnarl the same way the blue veins do on the backs of my hands. Near a mile long, each road, branching off in different directions only to meet at various points in between. I've traveled them a plenty and beyond.

But now that my days are longer, my legs won't carry the weight of me and if it weren't for my knees telling me when to slow down, my feet most certainly tell me when to stop. I sometimes forget, though, that I gotta go back and run outta steam before I mean to. So I wait before turnin' around. Might be on the bench of Mitchell Street. Maybe under the gumbo-limbo tree at Marimac Drive. Or maybe even along the stone wall of Cutter Road where Hook & Sinker sell their fishin' gear.

And I'll tell you what. I can look at that gear all afternoon, cause there was a time when I was right handy at nettin' a good day's catch. Ballyhoo, blue marlin, dolphin and pink snapper made many a fine supper. Agnes, the wife, had a way with fixin' fish. A little salt 'n pepper, lemon oil and herbs. Makes my mouth water just a thinkin' of what she'd done with that seafood. But that's neither here nor there now. Those days are long gone, just like Agnes, fine woman that she was.

Now a days I'm livin' with a daughter who can be a bit too fussy for my likin', but that's okay.

"Careful, Pops," she always says. "What if you get down the hill and get lost? What if you can't make it back up? I always worry and then I've got to come looking for you, don't you understand?"

Understand? What does she think I am? An absentminded old goat? Well old goats can get around, mind you and absentminded is just what I want to be right now. Why half the time I don't want to know what's goin' on. I just want to walk and wander and think about how nice it feels to step out on the road upright with my shoulders square. Why I'll go until tomorrow if need be, and by golly, she and nobody else is gonna stop me. Go ahead, little girly, worry. Cause I ain't. That's all behind me now.

Today I think I'll take Marimac Drive. It's about the straightest of the three roads and I ain't up for no meandering. Yep, clouds are good and movin' at a lumbering pace enough to shield the sun for about an hour or two. Takin' the hat, a wide-brimmed number whirly girly give me. Straw with a leather strap, good for when the wind kicks up. Girly can be good for sumpthin.

I tell her I'm off and where I'm headed as part of our agreement after several near all nighters on the bench at Mitchell Street. Good thing she finds me. That bench is hard and these old bones don't take too kindly to it. But usually by the time she finds me, I'm teary-eyed thinking of Agnes. Course, girly thinks it's on account that she's found me, so I just let her believe. My mistake. She'd never accept the notion I know what I'm doin' and had she never found me, I'd make it just nicely into sunrise and back home again. Thank you very much.

Besides, Mitchell Street is as harmless as a cat shelter given as it is with all the kids and dogs and cats of all sorts. Half the time I gotta shoo off some mutt who thinks he owns the world, but I been here longest and there's sure as heck no pooch big enough to stop me. 'Ceptin' maybe Dutch and he's tethered to a tree bigger than Manhattan. Big old bark. Sounds like a dynamite blast the way he waits till you're almost past then blows once, twice before bellowin' and snarlin'. Damn' near messed my drawers first time it happened. Who'd own such a beast? Why I oughta call the cops. Dutch is a menace to society.

So today, it's Marimac! A perfect day for it too, and I can easily make it down in short order given' me plenty of time for walking the docks. Maybe I'll see the Lady Slipper bobbin' in her berth, a beaute that one. About a fifty-five footer, I'd say. Mainsail with spinnaker, a true wind runner. Sleek and modern, decked out just fine. Why, what I'd give for a turn on the water on that one. Golly. Just the thought of her spurs me on.

But the hill is slick, an overnight rain has made it a bit tricky and I gotta watch every step. These old Sperry's ain't the best no more and the soles have lost some floorin'. Kinda like me, I guess. Worn in all the wrong places. Trusty things for the most part but good for probably only another couple a years. I focus on putting one foot in front of the other knowin' at least that as long as I do that, I'm one step closer to my goal. Down I travel, my gait uneven but purposeful.

Ms. Turner is waitin' I can tell. She's pretendin' to be workin' in her flowerbeds but I know what's what. She's a widow fifteen years now but likes to bat an eye at me. I should be flattered, I suppose. But she ain't no Agnes...she ain't no Dutch either so I reckon I can't tiptoe past and hope for the best now can I?

"Hello, Hap" she warbles. "On to the docks?"

"Yes ma'am. Gotta make my rounds."

"Of course you do. Might you want some tea in passing?"

Not today, Ms. Turner, but thank you kindly." And off I scamper as fast as I can at this age, wishin' instead I'd a taken Mitchell street and gambled on that damned dog. I'm not complainin' though. Ms. Turner is really kinda harmless. I just want to be alone.

Marimac levels out past Ms. Turner's and from here I can move more easily. The gumbo-limbo tree is three blocks down and there I'll stop to catch my breath beneath its sprawling branches and let my imagination go to work.

You see, pirates used to inhabit this area and tales of gold doubloons and treasure chests still scent the air. They used gumbo-limbo trees to etch directions to their buried treasures. E17 with a crooked arrow might indicate a treasure at seventeen paces to the East. A carved eye could be looking right at a site and a canoe might mean you have to row there. My gumbo-limbo has lots of etches—either from pirates or passions—your guess is as good as mine. But I like guessin' and might even confess to an etch or two myself just for the sake of addin' to the mystery. Hee hee.

For years now, I've imagined my treasure buried right along these parts put there by some dimwit who never returned. It is three feet to the right of the torchlight and about twenty feet below ground. It is, of course, filled with jewels, gold bars and money chains. Worth more than anything I can imagine. One day I intend to dig there, so today I'll add a new symbol. A skyward arrow. Why not? Haw! But I've left my penknife so it'll have to wait.

Instead, now that I'm here, I'll try to read all the other etches and make sense of 'em. An arrow pointing to the left faces three waves and the initials GTG. Could that mean Gaspar the Great sailed away with the treasure? Was there such a pirate? And what's that? A circle or a noose? I travel and finally sit next to AEM, Agnes Eileen Miller; put there by the pirate who'd stole her heart so many years ago. I sit with my hand against her bark. It's sooth and cool and just slightly knobby. My Agnes. My treasure. Buried. I will come for you. Today. Tomorrow. Soon.

Dreamin' I fall asleep.

When I wake, whirly girl is frantic and come to take me home and I'm all teary-eyed once again.

## Death Tower
Peter Huggins

Not the Hunger Tower
Made famous by Dante
In which Ugolino and his
Sons and grandsons
Starved. This concrete
Tower stood in Berlin
At the old divide
Between East and West
Where hundreds, perhaps
Thousands, were killed
By state-raised guards
Who shot their fellow
Citizens with the precision
Of surgeons, their deaths
A matter of little
Concern, enemies
Who deserved removal.
I look inside
The tower and it's hollow
All the way to the top

**Runaway**
David R. DiSiarro


She signaled for me to wait while she rolled
a cigarette, Connecticut shade tobacco smuggled
from the last five and dime in town, the dank poison
hidden in her bra. Her shape contorted around the corner
of the family colonial, a sad monument set back from the road,
idling against the heat, the residue, the etchings of our evenings
together. Outside the gravel driveway unfolded the discarded map

of America, veins and arteries surging through towns seldom seen,
through cities carved from concrete. What was left of us hit me
like a burst vessel, a road ahead, a steady onslaught of chain hotels,
billboards, free breakfasts, and the heavy eyelids of overnight
managers and maintenance workers, muttering obscenities
while little children looked on, mouths agape. Poor, pasty-legged
fathers, freed from slacks two or three weeks a year, poor mothers
eyeing the muscular groundskeepers, aching to be touched
in unfamiliar ways, both staring across a table, seeing how much a
person could erode, like the sliver of an eclipse, a rust stain
against the sky.

## Discovering My West African Ancestor
Suzette Bishop

You were there in my mother's black, wiry hair
she was ashamed of,
in the black hair my sister was born with,
falling out the next day,
my hair, blond as a child, but darkening,
darkening, and finally spiraling
with coconut oils.

You were why I was drawn
to the African imports store,
giraffe earrings and necklace,
lioness face painted on earrings,
gold and black details.
I bought them for you.

And when my husband asked me
about traveling and where I'd like to go,
nothing happened inside me
as he listed Caribbean islands,
England, Scotland, Sicily, Spain, Portugal.
I secretly saw savannah, watery
heat waves, rain trees, jeeps,
markets of colorful cloth, clay water jars.
I thought it was my love of wild animals.
But it was really you, wasn't it,
a memory or homesickness.

You had my mother read me the story
over and over, didn't you?
An escaped slave girl,

CONCLAVE

her solitary journey
protected by the night sky.
You were the one
who chose the first college
to admit African Americans,
part of the Underground Railroad,
a sculpture of railroad ties
jutting from the ground
outside my dorm room window.

I studied African American women's lit,
admiring their characters' escapes,
their mercy killings,
their survival instincts,
their self-possession
wrapped around their faces
like head scarves.
I found myself there
but didn't know why.

When the van left Pittsfield without us,
the hotel manager
where we tried to stay
called us prostitutes
because my friend was Black,
she shrugged, turning away.
But I cried knowing it was all he saw.
Your tears made him apologize,
letting us stay in the lobby,
bringing us donuts in the morning.

Everyone called the camp counselor
from the Ivory Coast a slut

who slept with all the male counselors.
I didn't care, her laugh,
her flawless skin, her hip-centered walk
drew me in, not away.

And there was Mabel's British accent
sparkling over the water,
mingled with your Scottish accent,
as we lounged on the dock
on our day off from the camp kitchen,
Mabel lean in her bikini,
telling me about visiting Nigeria,
her motherland.

And when the man from Ghana
invited me over for a traditional dinner,
plantains sliced lengthwise on the plate,
I didn't hesitate.

You led me to his bedroom,
my pale cream,
his coffee grounds' richness
mixed,
a noble prince of his tribe
you were denied having in slavery,
cornered by a noble Scotsman, instead.

He entered me twice that night—me and then you.

## Dream of Change
Chuma Mmeka

I have always dreamed
Of a Nigeria where all is well;
Where the streets are cleaned,
And everywhere is safe to dwell.

I have always dreamed
Of a Nigeria where promises are kept;
Where the leaders really want to lead,
Achieving results both brave and apt.

I have always dreamed
Of a Nigeria where peace and unity is secure;
Where tribal sentiment discords are doomed,
And terrorism and militancy become obscure.

Haven't you ever dreamed?
Of a Nigeria where children are cared for;
Where youths are skilled and well primed:
Patriotic, not brooding over a dark yore.

Feel free to dream with me -
Of a Nigeria where aged care is available;
Where social security is set and assured,
And Medicare is faithful and affordable.

In my dreams I see very clear -
A Nigeria where industries thrive;
Where electric power is effectively spread,
Where energy is accessed and refineries survive.

Truly I'm used to dreaming
Of a Nigeria where corruption is abominable;
Where common resources are fully harnessed,
And the system's process is due and infallible.

I have dreamed of change, till date, I still dream
Of an invigorated nation, an even greater Nigeria;
A realm where the common masses reign supreme,
But each time, some others put it down as malaria.

## If I Were in Charge of the World
Rachel Santellano

If I were in charge of the world, diseases, wars, cyber bullies,
and homeless people would not exist.

If I were in charge of the world there'd be world peace
and happiness.

If I were in charge of the world you would not have to worry
about global warming.
You would not have to pay a lot for gas.
You wouldn't have taxes or work on the weekends.
You wouldn't need good grades to go to college.

If I were in charge of the world fresh baked cookies would
be a vegetable.
Only fun pop songs would be on the radio.
And a person who forgot to do her homework could still be
in charge of the world.

(Rachel wrote this poem when she was eleven. She's now
fourteen.)

Spring 2016

Great stories
start here...

515 Spring St • Eureka Springs, AR
479.253.7444 • writerscolony.org

# We like your type!

Our residency program is open to writers of
every genre for short or long term stays.
Quiet, sequestered, inspirational – *and
affordable* – our individual writing suites are
designed to make your stay productive.
European style gourmet meals are served
Monday through Friday in the Colony
dining room, where you can share time with
other resident writers from around the globe.
Get away and write! For details, visit us
online at WritersColony.org

'The Writers' Colony
at Dairy Hollow

141

# Contributing Authors

**Lis Anna-Langston** is the recipient of many awards including; a 2013/2011 Pushcart nominee, 2014 Amazon Breakthrough Novel Semi-finalist, a five time WorldFest winner, FadeIn, Telluride IndieFest winner, Helene Wurlitzer Grant recipient, Chesterfield Film Project Finalist, New Century Writers winner and a finalist in the prestigious William Faulkner Competition. Her short films, screenplays, and novels have all been nominated and subsequently won awards including Best Novel and Best Short Film. She was awarded a quarter-finalist in the International Screenplay Awards, semi-finalist in the Nicholl Fellowships in Screenwriting, a quarter finalist in the Writers Network screenplay competition and First Place in The American Accolades Screenwriting Competition.

**Eleanor Leonne Bennett** is an internationally award-winning artist of over fifty awards. She was the CIWEM Young Environmental Photographer of The Year in 2013. Eleanor's photography has been published in *British Vogue* and *Harper's Bazaar*. Her work has been displayed around the world consistently for six years since the age of thirteen. This year (2015) she has done the anthology cover for the incredibly popular Austin International Poetry Festival.

**Suzette Bishop** teaches at Texas A&M International University. She has published three poetry books, most recently, *Hive-Mind*, and a chapbook. Her poems have appeared in many journals and anthologies and received Honorable Mention in the Pen 2 Paper Contest and first place in the *Spoon River Review* Poetry Contest.

**Jim Bohen** is a poet and songwriter/singer living in St. Paul, MN. His poems have appeared in the *Pinyon Review, the Minnesota Daily, the Red Paint Hill Poetry Journal, A Quiet Courage, Jenny* and elsewhere.

He seeks a publisher for his poetry manuscript *In Transit*. The music CD he produced, "Never Too Late," contains his vocals on 12 of the hundreds of songs he's written. (Samples can be heard at iTunes and cdbaby; search for "J B and the Phantom Band.")

**Yuan Changming** is a nine-time Pushcart nominee and author of six chapbooks, grew up in rural China, began to learn English at nineteen, and published monographs on translation before moving to Canada. With a PhD in English, Yuan currently edits *Poetry Pacific* with Allen Yuan in Vancouver, and has poetry appearing in *Best Canadian Poetry* (2009,12,14), *BestNewPoemsOnline, Cincinnati Review, Threepenny Review* and 1119 others across 37 countries.

**William C. Crawford** is a writer & photographer living in Winston-Salem, NC. He was a combat photojournalist in Vietnam. He later enjoyed a long career in social work. Crawdaddy also taught at UNC Chapel Hill. He photographs the trite, trivial, and the mundane. Crawford developed the forensic foraging technique of photography with his colleague, Sydney Lensman, Jim Provencher.

**David R. DiSarro** is currently an administrator and Assistant Professor of English at Endicott College in Beverly, MA. His work has previously appeared in The Wilderness House Literary Review, The Hawaii Pacific Review, Shot Glass Poetry Journal, The Ibbetson Street Magazine, The Orange Room Review, Third Wednesday, among others. His chapbook, I Used to Play in Bands, was recently published by Finishing Line Press. David currently lives on the North Shore of Massachusetts with his wife, Beth, boys Holden and Parker, and two rambunctious golden retrievers.

**Robert Fillman** is a Ph.D. candidate at Lehigh University in Bethlehem, PA, where he teaches English and edits the university's literary magazine, *Amaranth*. His poems have appeared or are forthcoming in *Apeiron Review*, *the Aurorean*, *The Chaffin Journal*, *The Chiron Review*, *Kudzu House Quarterly*, *Third Wednesday*, and others. He lives in eastern Pennsylvania with his wife, Melissa, and his two children, Emma and Robbie.

**Siaara Freeman** is an English education major with minors in both classical literature (archaic Egyptian/Greek/Roman/ focus) and creative writing, who bartends part time while being a travelling/slamming spoken word ninja when time permits. Currently she just wants to be an artist, her artological clock is ticking. At the age of 17, she shared the stage with the late, beloved poetess Maya Angelou. She participated in the national teen competition Brave New Voices 2007 (making finals stage her first year) 2008 and 2009. She become grand slam champion of Cleveland and Columbus, Ohio. Siaara's poetry takes a very honest outlook from the life of a woman being black, lesbian and urban.

**Elaine Gallant** lives, loves and is still surprised that life has landed her in Hawaii. Once a freelance golf, travel, and tennis writer with a BA in Journalism from the University of Central Florida, her work has appeared in *Golf Orlando*, *Golf for Women*, Travelgolf.com, and other online publications. She has since entered the more complicated world of fiction.

**Peter Huggins**'s books of poetry are *Audubon's Engraver*, *South*, shortlisted for the International Rubery Award, *Necessary Acts*, *Blue Angels*, and *Hard Facts*. He is also the author of a picture book, *Trosclair and the Alligator*, which has appeared on the PBS show Between the Lions, and a middle grade novel, *In the Company of Owls*. He teaches in the English Department at Auburn University.

**Mike Koenig** received his MFA in Creative Writing & Publishing Arts from the University of Baltimore. He currently lives in Columbia, Maryland and works for Discovery Communications. His fiction can be seen in *Phoebe, Quiddity, Clover, Kestrel, and The Tulane Review.*

**Ken Leland** won the 2015 Creative Writing prize from the English Department at Carleton University. His fiction, both long and short, often depicts Canadian or American settings, First Nations, Black Loyalists and Quakers. There is also a series of northern Indiana stories set in rural and small towns; four of those stories have been published by Prolific Press in their Inwood collections. The author's first historical novel was published in 2013 by Fireship Press and is titled *1812 The Land Between Flowing Waters.* Leland can be contacted through his website at: www.kenlelandauthor.com

**Maria Elena B. Mahler**'s work has been published in English and Spanish. Her first bilingual poetry collection, *Sweeping Fossils,* is forthcoming by Glass Lyre Press in 2016. Maria Elena also co-authored the non-fiction book *The Heart of Health* (Truth Publishing Co. 2011). She is the editor of the poetry anthology *Woman in Metaphor* (NHH Press 2013), a collection of 27 poets from around the world inspired by the paintings of Stephen Linsteadt. Maria Elena was raised in the South of Chile. After graduating with a degree in Communications, she lived and worked in Mexico and Canada, and currently resides in the Sonoran Desert of Southern California.

**Shahé Mankerian**'s most recent manuscript, *History of Forgetfulness*, has been a finalist at four prestigious competitions: the 2013 Crab Orchard Series in Poetry Open Competition, the 2013 Bibby First Book Competition, the *Quercus Review Press*, Fall Poetry

Book Award, 2013, and the 2014 White Pine Press Poetry Prize. His poems have appeared in *Mizna*.

**Jenny McBride**'s poems have appeared in *The California Quarterly, Blast Furnace, Green Social Thought*, and other journals. She has also published fiction.

**Susheela Menon** was born in India and teaches Creative Writing in Singapore. One of her latest essays appeared in Kitaab, a publishing house based in Singapore.

**Chuma Mmeka** is a multi-talented and versatile Nigerian. He is a new-generation African poet, writer and author of several published books; he is a successful movie actor in and a dedicated altruist with successful landmark activities. Married to Nikky Mmeka with lovely children Eby and Amy, Chuma Mmeka also known as "T-char" has a background in Law and other fields. Born a Christian, Chuma dubs himself 'freethinker' and 'realist'. He has a favorite pitch: "Never force it, just set it on course." He takes life just one step at a time.

**Toti O'Brien** was born in Rome and lives in Los Angeles. Her work has appeared in *Litro NY, Sein und Verden, Synestesia* and *Lost Coast*, among other journals and anthologies.

**Pattie Palmer-Baker** is artist and poet. Although she combines these two forms of expression in collages of paste paper and calligraphy, the inspiration for and the meaning of the artwork lies within the poem. Nominated for the Pushcart Poetry Prize in 2013 Published in: *Eholi Gaduji Journal, Poeming Pigeons Anthology, Petals in the Pan Anthology, Silver Birch Press Blog, The Ghazal Page*, and *Voicecatcher*.

**Olfa Philo** (Drid) is an ex-international volleyball player, an

English teacher, a PhD scholar and a committed poetess from Tunisia whose cause is wording and unveiling the buried emotions and phobias of the oppressed and the downtrodden. A female rebel at heart who wages war against injustice, intimidation, objectification, subjugation and violence against the 'inferior,' powerless and 'Othered' groups. Her poems appeared in different online and print literary journals. She was also featured by the *American HyperTexts Journal* in its spotlight rubric. After gaining recognition from different international reviews, she has recently published her first collection of poetry entitled *(Un)jailed*. She also published a play entitled "Sublime Revenge."

**Kenneth Pobo** had two books out in 2015: *Bend of Quiet from Blue Light Press* and *Booking Rooms in the Kuiper Belt* from Urban Farmhouse Press. He teaches creative writing and English at Widener University in Pennsylvania.

**Rachel Santellano** is a fourteen-year-old high school student who lives in a suburb of Chicago. She wrote this poem when she was eleven.

**Rikki Santer** is an award-winning poet whose work has appeared in numerous publications including *Ms. Magazine, Poetry East, Margie, Crab Orchard Review, Grimm* and *The Main Street Rag*. Her four published poetry collections are: *Front Nine, Kahiki Redux, Clothesline Logic*, and *Fishing for Rabbits*. She currently lives in Columbus, Ohio where she teaches literature, writing, and film studies. www.rikkisanter.com

**Jeremy Schnee** lives in Portland, Oregon. Aside from writing, he likes to garden, practice martial arts, and spend time with his family. His fiction has been published in Dark Corners, New Plains Review, and Exit 7. He recently completed writing his first novel.

For more information about his stories, and to read articles on the topic of writing, please visit www.jeremyschnee.com.

**Louis Staeble** lives in Bowling Green, Ohio. His photographs have appeared in *Agave, Blinders Journal, Blue Hour, Digital Papercut, Elsewhere Magazine, Fifth Wednesday Journal, Four Ties Literary Review, Inklette Magazine, Microfiction Monday, Paper Tape Magazine, Qwerty, Revolution John, Rose Red Review, Sonder Review, Timber Journal, Up The Staircase Quarterly* and *Your Impossible Voice.*

**Marjorie Stelmach**'s fourth volume of poems is *Without Angels* (Mayapple, 2014). Previous volumes include *A History of Disappearance* and *Bent upon Light* (Tampa). Recent work has appeared in *Boulevard, Cincinnati Review, Gettysburg Review, Image, New Letters*, and others. She lives in St. Louis, Missouri.

**Dallas Woodburn** is a recent Steinbeck Fellow in Creative Writing and a three-time Pushcart Prize nominee. She has published fiction and nonfiction in Zyzzyva, Fourth River, Prism Review, The Los Angeles Times, and North Dakota Quarterly, and her short story collection was a finalist for the Flannery O'Connor Award for Short Fiction and the Augury Books Prose Award. She is the founder of Write On! For Literacy, an organization that empowers youth through reading and writing endeavors: www.writeonbooks.org.

**Daniel Wu** is a sophomore at the University of Michigan studying environmental engineering. His work has been selected as a finalist five times for the Arts@Umich photography competition and he has previously been published in Inklette magazine.

# In the Fall 2016 Issue

## Carl Sennhenn Poetry Prize 2016
## Rilla Askew Short Fiction Prize 2016

Winners will receive a $500 cash prize as well as publication in *Conclave*.

We will accept entries of unpublished poetry and short fiction until July 30, 2016. There are no limitations in form or content. Simultaneous submissions are permitted, but if your work is accepted elsewhere, we cannot refund your contest entry. You are welcome to enter as many times as you wish. Only submit original work that has not appeared in any form, online or in print, or won any previous awards. All manuscripts will be read "blind." English work only. Finalists will be selected by the editorial staff and prominent writers acting as contest judges.

If you have questions, please visit our website:
http://www.conclavejournal.com

To submit work to these contests, visit:
https://balkanpress.submittable.com/

# Take Your Writing to the Next Level

## William Bernhardt Summer Writing Retreats 2016

William Bernhardt (Publisher of *Conclave,* author of the Red Sneakers Writers Book series) is one of the most in-demand writing instructors in the nation, regularly appearing on the faculty at conferences in Hawaii, New York, and other venues. Bernhardt also hosts small-group workshops for aspiring writers struggling with a work-in-progress. Each retreat consists of several intense, inspiring days learning the art and craft of writing with hands-on instruction, exercises, discussions of writing issues, editing, and advice specifically addressing each participant's work-in-progress.

**May 18-22, 2016** Eureka Springs AR, The Writers Colony at Dairy Hollow
**June 9-12, 2016** Nashua NH (Boston area), Crowne Plaza Nashua
**June 23-26, 2016** Huntington Beach (Anaheim) CA, Mystery Ink
**June 30-July 3, 2016** Durango Colorado
**July 21-24, 2016** Oahu, Hawaii

For more information, visit:
http://www.williambernhardt.com/red_sneaker_wc/writing_retreats.php